HEROIC DisGRACE

Order out of chaos. Hope out of fear.
A **WORSHIP HERO** STORY

SCOTT W. BOX

HEROIC DisGRACE

©Scott W. Box

Print ISBN: 978-1-09839-720-3

eBook ISBN: 978-1-09839-721-0

CONTENTS

FOREWORD

Mental health has garnered a lot of attention over the last few years. It seems like every few months, the news media shares yet another dramatic headline of a suicide taken place. A pastor, an actor, musician, or sports hero—we've heard it all. Even in our own neighborhoods: a tragic suicide from our kids' school, our workplace, a neighbor. Maybe even someone in our own family. It's impossible for us to escape, and unfortunately, I've experienced it personally in my industry. Back in 2017, a friend of ours named *Chester Bennington* from the rock band *Linkin Park* took his own life. What was even more jaw-dropping was just two months prior, Chester's good friend *Chris Cornell* from the rock band *Soundgarden* died by suicide as well. When it was revealed that Chester's death took place on Chris Cornell's birthday, I completely lost it. I feared the worst: that fans worldwide may start to copy their actions. To say it sent shockwaves throughout the music industry would be an enormous understatement. It felt like the news shook the entire world. Fans of music, not just rock music, but fans of all genres of music, took to social media to mourn the musician's deaths. But it went further than that. It felt to me like these two suicides, so closely connected, ignited a massive wake-up call for the world to start a real conversation regarding mental health and deal with the stigma associated with it.

Mental illness does not discriminate. Regardless of an individual's identity—sex, ethnicity, age, social class, environment—experts report that close to half of all Americans will battle with some form of mental illness. So what is causing this epidemic? There are many forms of mental sickness, but I believe a massive identity crisis is one of the biggest causes of this depression-induced dark cloud over much of humanity. Undeniably, more and more people are starting to wake up and realize that chasing the wrong things in life does not work. I believe the antidote is found through discovery; discovering our identities in Jesus Christ develops the strong character we need to handle the pressures of life. I believe Jesus is the first step in combating the plague of depression and hopelessness.

I love that Jesus doesn't sugarcoat his message in the Bible. He tells it like it is! We have been given the promise from Christ that we will, without a doubt, face many tribulations in this life. However, Jesus has also assured us that He will always be with us in our pain if we give him the reins and let Him walk with us through our sufferings—which in turn always leads to healing, peace, joy, and comfort.

Maybe you don't know me from Adam, and you're wondering how I sound so confident this will work.

Glad you asked.

I, personally, have lived through the dramatic effects of the "Christ within" reality as I watched Jesus flip everything around in my life from total darkness to absolute health and wellness of mind, body, and soul - including my very own struggles with major depression.

As you will soon read in *Heroic Disgrace*, my cousin, Scott Box, has experienced this dramatic reconstruction in his own life as well, but in his unique way. That's another thing I love about Jesus. He moves in people's lives in similar ways while using many different techniques to accomplish His purposes in us.

The message is clear: we exist in a world with many pitfalls that any of us can fall into at any second; every living person will suffer a form of depression or mental illness at some point in their life. Nobody is exempt from suffering, which is precisely why we need to share our stories of how we've overcome our personal obstacles. Scott has done an outstanding job at doing just that with *Heroic Disgrace*. So get ready to have your minds blown when you learn of the courage and fortitude Scott had to find deep within himself, along with his loving family and friends, that God so obviously placed in his life to help him.

Heroic Disgrace is truly a remarkable story about one man's fight to find authentic freedom. I am extremely confident that this book will change many lives.

It's one of the best stories I've read in a long time.

And I'm not just saying that because Scott Box is my cousin :)

Enjoy.

—Brian "Head" Welch, co-founder of the *Grammy Award* winning band *Korn* and *New York Times* best-selling author of *Save Me From Myself*

BEFORE THE STORY BEGINS

I wrote my story, to inspire each of us to mold our habits around a vision of new life and endless adventure, to see God's path through our challenges—and always with an eternal perspective. My goal is not to inspire perfection or create theologians. My goal is to cheer you on as you learn to live your story as a heroic worshiper of Jesus Christ. Maybe you'll cheer me on in the same way—that we'll become heroic as Jesus is heroic. I trust the story that follows will help us begin to accomplish our unending adventure-filled, heroic purpose together.

—Scott Wilson Box. July 2021

"The LORD your God who goes before you, will Himself, fight on your behalf..."—Deuteronomy 1:30

SUPERHERO

Boy Scout Vol. 1

As far as I know, my dad never owned an official "HERO" badge. I know he never earned or owned something like an Eagle Scout badge either, but that didn't stop him. Like any good all-American Boy Scout, Dad could assess dangerous or chaotic situations, discern people with noble or villainous intentions, make decisions, and take action fast. It happened often.

One night when I was a young teenager, I was sleeping downstairs on the floor of my dad's office. I had been kindly kicked out of my room to allow my brother's friend to bunk with him in our bedroom upstairs. I remember moving the cushions from our family room couch to Dad's office floor and laying out a sheet and a couple of blankets. It had excited me to be able to open the window in Dad's office that evening for some fresh cool summer air. So that's exactly where I created my makeshift bed, directly beneath that window, laid down, threw the blankets over me, and slipped quickly and peacefully into dreamland.

It was two, maybe three hours later—in the middle of the night— when I was jolted awake by violent banging that seemed to have been coming from every direction and savage, bloodthirsty yelling coming from a voice only a few feet from my head outside the window.

The feeling of terror chasing me out of my sleep was overwhelming. "Dad, Dad, Dad . . ." was all the adrenaline would permit my mind to scream as I involuntarily and immediately ran out the office door, directly past the booming along the front of the house, up the house's stairs, only to have been greeted by Dad at the top stair. He was in his tight and white undies and nothing else. As far as he knew, in the dark, I was the thunderous invader.

As I approached the top stair, Dad had his right arm cocked and his left arm outstretched in my face in utter defiance. With a Viking-like yell and the only time in his life Dad punched me, he pulled back his outstretched arm and drilled the palm of his cocked hand into the nook between my eyes and my nose, just below my forehead. My head popped back, and my body followed it. I would have certainly tumbled down the stairs I'd just climbed except for, because of Dad's athletic instincts and (almost) immediate recognition I was his son, not the invader, he leaned, reached, and caught my shoulder. Dad steadied me. Then in one smooth motion he shoved me to the floor at the top stair. I collapsed without debate, uselessly shaking my head to try to clear the pouring, reflexive tears from my eyes. In fact, my immediate quarrel was with the hashtags, exclamation points, question marks and birdies circling my head. I'd forgotten why I was on the stairs in the first place honestly.

I was sniffing the running snot back into my nose while Dad made no other sound. I was confused, entirely dazed. But Dad was standing above me with complete composure. He stood still. He was pausing and listening. With his hand firmly resting on my head—a comforting reassurance—Dad was keeping me seated.

In that house, the front door was directly below the stairs. It was still booming. A male voice was in hysterics outside. In total contrast, Dad wasn't even breathing hard. Though I couldn't see his eyes, only his glowing white underwear, I felt Dad's hand flick past my tall, messy, bed-head hair as he moved back to his room, "Scott, stay calm. Stay down. I got this." Still blinking and snorting back snot I thought, I sure as heck don't "got this." Dad believed he did . . . whatever that meant. So I blinked and squinted to see the front door down the dark stairway while I wiped away the leaks that had sprung from my eyes.

Dad moved quickly to the window in his room above the front door—from my position at the top of the stairs, I could see both Dad and the front door—and without skipping a beat, He calmly spoke out an open second-story window:

"Sir, you have less than three seconds before I shoot you in the head. If I happen to miss, I reload fast. I will kill you twice. Start talking."

There was a single and sudden muffled sound against the front door. I squinted from the top stair leaning from where I was watching Dad to make sure I could raise the alarm when the destruction of the front door happened. It didn't. The muffled sound was the blunt thump of a body pressed hard against the door to shelter itself from the rain of bullets about to be discharged from ten feet above. There was a very brief awkward silence. Then I heard the sound of a man's voice. Indistinct at first, it grew quickly in volume and urgency. Straining to hear what was said, I listened close:

"Fire. No! Don't fire! I mean, it's a fire. I'm on fire. No, my house is on fire. Please don't fire, Tom, I'm your neighbor, Ed. Help me. What do I do? Tom, please don't shoot. Help me put out the fire!"

Boy Scout Vol. 2

Saying nothing and moving away from the window, Dad left Ed in suspense. Having already pulled on his blue jeans, Dad skipped a shirt and instead pulled his thermal half-zip sweatshirt over his belly. Dad blasted down the stairs like lightning. Cautiously keeping his pistol pointed at waist level as he opened the door to a hysterical neighbor, Dad kept the gun hidden behind the door. From my view at the top of the stairs, I could see the yellow and orange flicker from the flames of a legit fire off Ed's left cheek and forehead. "Scott. Call. Here." is all Dad said as he leaned over, set the pistol on the first step and rushed out the door, leaving the door wide open. I knew what that meant. I ran down the stairs, first grabbing the gun. I turned the corner and headed down the hall to pick up the phone. I called 911 while I was emptying the five bullets from the revolver. Dad always left the first chamber empty. I set the empty gun on Mom's decorative plates in the kitchen cabinets above the microwave oven and rushed to put my clothes on.

I bolted out the front door, flicking the door closed behind me. From Ed's side yard, Dad yelled at me to turn around and bring the garden hose. I hit the brakes and made it quickly back to the hose. It wasn't until I started to lift the hose out of its holder that I realized the five .38-caliber bullets were still in my left hand. I'd kept them in my fist as I dressed. I shoved the bullets into my pocket to free both hands to drag out our extra-long hose into the yard.

After turning the hose faucet on, I struggled to free the hose from the various yard and garden decorations. Pulling a heavy hose full of water across the grass was ridiculously hard . . . and stupid. I was panicking and I knew it.

Eventually, I thought I was free and clear, so I clutched the hose, turned, and bolted into a run. I made it less than ten or fifteen feet before I got yanked backward like a yo-yo onto my butt, arms and legs splayed, completely laid out. The heavy hose dropped in a tangled heap right onto my crotch. I gagged twice while trying to fight off the stomach-turning queasiness of taking a hit like that to my...tenders. Somehow, the hose had gotten knotted behind me anyway.

My body involuntarily wretched a couple more times as I lifted the hose again to carry it the remaining distance. Belatedly, I did get the long extended hose to Ed's house. But by that time, even though they were still a long way off, I could finally hear the fire engines' sirens approaching.

As I had been bringing the hose, I had pushed through some thorny blackberry bushes that grabbed at my arms and legs. I hardly noticed the thorns, and my nausea had instantaneously disappeared as I witnessed Dad kick in the external side door to Ed's garage, exposing a wall of flames between the garage and the house. I fell to the ground breathing as fast as a hummingbird flaps its wings.

Grabbing the hose nozzle from beside me and shoving it into Ed's hands, Dad calmly told Ed to keep a constant spray going over his shoulder, "Keep the flames off me, Ed." Then equipped with Ed's garden hose, Dad crawled on his belly just a few feet through the bashed-in door and into the burning garage, assessing the risks and potential for success.

He must have felt good enough about his options because Dad let the water from the hose he was holding loose without any other words. As he started spraying water from his hose along the wall of flame, I saw arching blasts of sparks from newly exposed wires. Black smoke and the pop and sizzle of fire began hissing loudly and consistently as the water Dad was spraying onto the wall across the garage turned instantly to steam. Steam and smoke began mixing. It was only a brief observation—the smoke now flickered much grayer in the quick flash of the flames. The flames from under the garage's eaves illuminated the smoke rolling out the door. In a constant flow, it rolled above the roofline and into the night sky.

A never-ending chatterbox of "Oh God. What did I do?" and "Patty's going to kill me!" then "You're still alive in there, right Tom?" Ed was on feverish verbal repeat while Dad was doing his best to keep the fire from breaching the garage wall into the house long enough for the professionals to arrive. With the risk of electrocution becoming ever higher as more and more wires were exposed and water began to pool around him, Dad eventually inched himself backward and out the door. He was drenched, coughing, and almost overcome with heat and smoke. The firemen took command.

The whole experience bent my mind a little. My dad was a dazzling champion and guardian deliverer. He was every bit a hero as the cool-looking firemen who took over the saving of Ed's house that night. (Ed had mistakenly thrown hot coals from his barbecue into the trash in his garage before going to bed.)

With a raspy voice, Dad sent me home to put the hose away, properly store his revolver, nurse my loins, and wait for him. He helped Ed work things out with the firemen and finish the emergency call before coming home soaked and smelling all sorts of wrong. Dad had been amazing under pressure. I was struck by him that night—in more ways than one—with the bruises around my nose and eyes, as well as my sore neck and butt, proving it.

After Dad and I grunted our way through a small debriefing, he took a shower and went back to bed. In the meantime, I stripped down to my own tighty-whities and gingerly crawled back into my sleeping bag on the floor of Dad's office, right where it all started.

This story is an excellent singular example of the types of things in which I grew up believing were heroic. I saw Dad do stuff like this numerous times. He pulled off terrific things to help people. Tom Box saved the day. He didn't talk about it. Dad just did it. He modeled it. He modeled service. He modeled heroism. Heck, even my dad's prayers sounded heroic to me. Dad was outwardly humble, but he oozed charisma and could back it up.

No, Dad didn't carry a badge that read "HERO." Although, it wouldn't have surprised me if he had an invisible badge fastened to his chest.

Billy-Club-Toting

For Dad, the groundwork for his operational definition of heroic things had been laid as a child. Generations of Box family members dedicated themselves to living lives of duty and honor. Maybe the best way to explain it was that the Boxes were traditional all-American, God-fearing public servants by trade. My great-grandfather on my dad's side, Billie Box Sr., was a Texas-born boy who grew to 6'6" and walked a "beat" in downtown Los Angeles; a career billy-club-toting policeman during the 1920s and '30s. There are fantastic stories about how Great-Grandpa Box policed his beat in Los Angeles that make me smile, puff out my chest and flex my muscles a bit. Later in the early 1940s, he was one of a handful of officers who became the first CHiPs (California Highway Patrol) riding the meaty-looking and sounding Harley-Davidson motorcycles. He was one tough man.

Billie Sr. and Loma Box had one child, Billie Box Jr. As he became an adult, Billie Jr. joined the merchant marines and sailed beneath the Golden Gate Bridge out of San Francisco to fight communism in Korea. Returning from the war to his wife and son—my dad—Grandpa Box followed in his father's footsteps and joined the California Highway Patrol. On and on the stories go from there.

See, Dad and I were born into a blood and guts, cops and robbers, cowboys and Indians family. How could I blame myself for whatever operational definition of hero I developed as a child and later carried into adulthood? I couldn't. I had to blame my dad and mom, my grandpa and grandma, and both sets of my great-grandparents on my dad's side. I also had to blame the astoundingly good—not perfect, but good—country of the United States of America and the cultural Christian faith that produced each of those people in my family. Sure, their motivations may or may not have been from the same humble or selfless place, but the drive to be heroic was in every one of these men and women.

For better or worse, I was born into swashbuckling, red-blooded, ambitious, all-American, God-fearing, Box bravado refined by powerful traditional models of selfless service. No apologies.

Patton Vol. 1

Clergyman: "I was interested to see a Bible by your bed. You actually find time to read it?"

General Patton: "I sure do! Every g——damn day."

In early May 1970, my dad took my mom to see the eventual "Best Picture" Oscar-winning biographical war movie Patton. It was their first date. Good for Dad, as he got the gory "guy" film and the girl. Good for Mom, since she loved him anyway.

In Dad's defense, before the movie, he did take Mom to the famous Tick Tock restaurant in Hollywood for dinner and then two blocks west, down Hollywood Boulevard to Hollywood Pantages Theatre for the movie. Mom didn't care; she was blown away that Tom Box thought she was special enough to take her on a date.

Mom was smitten by the very popular 6'4" skinny redhead senior varsity basketball player from Redondo Union High School. But as romantic and special as their love story was, this particular story wasn't so much about their love for each other, but rather my dad's love for all things he perceived as genuinely heroic: loyalty; duty; honor; and all-American, God-fearing, backbone and ballsiness.

Put bluntly, Mom had no idea just how influential the movie she would watch that night would become to her future husband, and later, her future son, Scott Wilson Box.

Patton Vol. 2

There was some inspired magic in George C. Scott's portrayal of United States General Patton that drew me in from the movie's first words. For Dad, until the 1986 movie Top Gun came along, there was no opening of a film that ranked higher in his mind. Patton's character addresses an unseen crowd of soldiers after walking in front of a gigantic American flag. Here was exactly how the movie Patton began:

> "Be seated. Now, I want you to remember that no bastard ever won a war by dying for his country. He won it by making the other poor dumb bastard die for his country."

On and on, Patton spoke for a full five minutes in the same candid and crass way he started. To capture the tone and spirit of his message, I minimized his talk to that most tame fraction.

Patton was a polarizing figure, much like a modern-day Donald Trump—people either loved or hated Patton. And after Patton gave this speech in 1945, people worldwide were shocked by his vulgarity. Newspapers had a heyday. The United States military had already had its hands full of and disciplined Patton multiple times. But he was an arrogant, obscene genius, and it was wartime. The military needed Patton; It was a time for heroes, even vulgar ones.

It may have been crude, even profane, but a call to arms like General Patton's unified warriors to a singular cause. Patton didn't beg or plead for unity. Patton knew that people were required to set aside preferences and opinions to unite against evil throughout history. Patton's speech unified more than anything else because he called upon the divine heroic design and duty within his men and all people. He knew his audience too. Besides that, he was a winner. His men wanted to follow a winner into battle. People still do.

Patton was going to fight the wartime Axis darkness whether others came with him or not—it was his duty, and everybody knew it. People were critical, but Americans were united in their gladness General Patton was on their side, not the Axis's.

So, after watching this movie as a boy, I wanted to go kill me some Nazis. No! That's a total exaggeration. But there *was* something inside me that remained deeply attracted to this type of motivation. It worked on me. I was stirred to passionate common-sense rally cries like this.

> *The fight against adversity, tragedy, and evil required all-American, God-fearing people to do their duty and act like heroes.*

No, General Patton didn't have true heroism figured out, but he got closer than many people. Dad and I agreed.

Lucky You

Real life, real drama, and real history; a great love story brought two families together in my mom, Janice Scott, and my dad, Tom Box. So it's kind of a fascinating fact that Mom decided my name almost exactly twenty-four months before I was born.

While Mom was standing at the wedding altar with Dad and the pastor on the day of their wedding, the moment the pastor offered his greeting to the people who were in attendance, "Welcome to the Scott/Box Wedding," she thought, Oh, that's a really good name for a son!

. . . And that, friends, was how the world got me. Well, not technically, but you get the point. Lucky you.

Hero Duty Vol. 1

From my perspective as an eight to thirteen-year-old boy, the glitz of Hollywood and Southern California never stopped sprinkling itself on our family. From movie stars, sports stars, famous pastors like Chuck Swindoll, and Christian teachers like James Dobson, to Disneyland and Knott's Berry Farm, to the Los Angeles Lakers and Los Angeles Dodgers winning multiple championships, I had stars in my eyes. And from my multiple undefeated successes on sports teams with my dad as my coach, you might imagine I learned to believe in a particular idea of hero and the hero's duty. You'd be right.

My idea of "heroes are winners" would follow me for twenty-five, maybe thirty years. The influence of a General Patton-like heroism had a magnetic pull that was very, very hard to escape.

Heck, my dad worked for the Christian marketing company supporting Doctor James Dobson and Focus on the Family. Focus on the Family was absolutely heroic in executing its mission, and I knew it. They were winners. Dad talked to me about all of the heroic things they were engaged in, exciting things for Jesus. There was a ton of pride involved with Dad's work.

The thing was, my youngest days of belief in the hero concept grew as a result of massive and concentrated doses of 1980s Southern Californian affluence, presentation, and abundance repeatedly heaped on my family—and lots and lots of victories. All this happened when I was most impressionable. In work and play, heroes were winners.

So yeah, while people say Hollywood living is shallow and hollow in almost every way, I remember it all very fondly, especially now as an adult. I'd go so far as to say those were great years.

The crazy twist was, even if those Hollywood things weren't exactly "real," they were real to me.

As I consider my story, my all-American, God-fearing sense of hero duty had been framed by all sorts of other real-life forces. Disappointingly, this was how *my context about heroism only got me halfway to true heroism.* This shortfall proved to be a magnet that would attract all sorts of other ideas of heroism to fill in the gaps and create a monster a bit like Frankenstein's creation, handicapping me significantly in the years to come.

Ultimately, heroism in the Box family was a charge, a necessity. It made us American statesmen of sorts. And everyone should have been a statesman. Heroism was a tradition passed from one generation to the next. Heroism was my absolute duty.

SUPERBhuman

Like any normal boy, I thought about becoming a hero and saving the day all the time in my childhood. But unlike many boys I knew, I didn't want to escape the attention of people in authority. I wouldn't shy away from recognition and expectation either. I didn't want to fly under anyone's radar. So I didn't. Heroic? I believed I would grow up to be heroic.

Scott Wilson Box was born to be a hero.

But I would be lying if I didn't say I believed I would live my life with a larger figurative cape flowing in the wind behind me than the average person. The key was not ever to be arrogant about it, but instead to be sincere and determined about it.

I knew I would need to work to rise high, high above a C or B grade, and become a "superbhuman." I was not above working hard for the honor. And I was game to meet and exceed the expectation. I hated not getting A's on my report card or on any assessment. I needed to be great at it all. I set out to achieve superb status during my lifelong heroic quest. All-American, God-fearing superb status was a part of the responsibility, part of the formula for holding the line.

The expected outcome of my sincere heroic determination was I would get what I had earned or deserved from my adoring fans. My expectation was that good guys like me were to be recognized, accepted or respected, and rewarded. Luke and Han got medals from the princess at the end of Star Wars. Harry Potter gained back the respect of the entire wizarding world by finally, heroically, defeating Voldemort. Even a dead hero like "Goose" had his dog tags respectfully thrown out into the ocean by his best friend "Maverick" in Top Gun.

Heroes got what they deserved in all the stories I loved. Superbhumans were entitled to glory and honor, and riches and remembrance.

So as a young boy, my thought was never if I would become a hero. I only ever believed I would become a hero in a meaningful story. I thought it was everyone else's duty to pay close attention to me. I paid close attention to them. But I naively did not consider other people; many people in my generation and many of my parent's generation were beginning to see heroism differently than I did. I found out the hard way; not everyone appreciated or accepted my all-American, God-fearing version of heroism.

Beating Up Baddies Vol. 1

Growing up in Southern California through my elementary school years, my friends at school and I played a game we called wall ball. The game may be known by many other names, but it was played with a simple rubber, inflatable playground ball about the same size as a basketball. We played the game against a large wooden wall out on the school playground. I suspect local rules—how the game is played—reign supreme in a game like wall ball. But our Sunset Lane Elementary version allowed an antsy boy like me to expend a lot of energy and school-day agitation even in a short recess. Most of the time, everything played out smoothly. We had the routine down pat.

However, there was one afternoon during recess, after the mad dash to line up and start the game, one of the sixth-grade bad guys (bullies) paraded out from the shadows of the covered lunch area with his two or three minions. The older kids' recess overlapped the younger children's for about five minutes or so.

That day, those older boys roughly shoved their way into the line directly in front of the girl I had a crush on. Tossing her aside, she tripped without a sound but fell hard to the ground scraping her knees and palms. She stood up bloody and, as if she was at fault, limped back in line behind the giggling bullies with her chin resting on her chest. It broke my heart. I wanted justice.

So, after taking a quick look around, I walked past the lame minions, straight up to the big baddie, said nothing, and punched him as hard as I could in the stomach. He dropped to the hot pavement, gagging. I reached down and dragged him to the end of the line. All of a sudden, he started squealing like a chubby pig, his minions scattering back to the shadows. Justice was served. I went back to my place in line as if nothing happened. It all happened just like it would in a television show.

But because of the big baddy's reaction, two of the playground supervisor ladies were on the scene in no time. The kid bully had begun to scream while drawing circles on the hot blacktop with his butt, looking for shade that did not exist. Oh, the drama. Frankly, he was twitching as if I'd decapitated him. Whatever attention he wanted, he got it.

"Which one of you violent boys did this to this soul!" was the glaring question posed over and over by a fuming adult playground volunteer, in between nonstop blasts from her whistle. I thought, She just called that kid, "this soul?" I knew what she was asking. It was pretty darn obvious. But I wanted to correct her, "He has no soul. He is only a pig turd." I didn't. But it was a cliché in every way. Then, even more formulaic, every kid took a step back, and I was left standing alone with the girl I'd defended. I did not expect all the other witnesses to be such rats and turn me in with such immediacy. Grrr.

Well, I might as well have been a bomb, and the two women were the bomb squad rushing to defuse the "Scott Box bomb." One lady sped me off the playground. One lady stayed with the oinking bully. No one attended to my "girl" friend.

I was dragged by the collar back into my classroom by a fuming volunteer who hated redheaded boys, I guess. Entering my studentless classroom, I received the verbal equivalent of a tar and feathering from squawking parrots pointing their wings and flapping in heated circles around me. My teacher and the playground lady had turned into birds of prey. I was their afternoon snack. I was so stunned by their response. I couldn't answer. I only cried. It was as if nothing else was taken into account. Did they not recognize the bully I had stood up to was two years older and two heads taller than me? Did they not even look at his face and realize he was the same one bringing dirty magazines to share with his friends on the playground? Did they not even care that he was involved in some altercation nearly every week, and he was always the one standing over some other helpless kid? Somehow, I'd become the villain, not the hero.

Agonizingly, I went home shamed for being such a "violent boy." I also remember the word "pathetic" being a word I didn't yet know but heard from my teacher's mouth that day. She gave me an official disciplinary pink slip as well as a sealed note to share with my parents. I was sick to my stomach as if I'd been the one punched.

Maybe my actions defending my friend were wrong. But to me, it seemed a measured and acceptable response to a wrong. Regardless, I had genuinely tried to set things right. I believed I was a good guy restoring order to chaos. Sadly, chaos came looking for me. Chaos put me back on my heels. I didn't think this thought specifically, but I know I felt it: *Where was the glory, honor, and riches?* I also wondered, would the perception of others, people in authority or power, cause me to now be remembered as violent and pathetic instead of good and kind?

The Confession

That heated experience happened on a beautiful, warm spring Friday afternoon. And I was too fearful of saying anything about it to Mom and Dad until the next morning. I had slept terribly that night, knowing I still had to show my parents the pink slip and the note.

Understandably, my conscience wouldn't allow me to sleep in, so I got up early that Saturday morning, pushed my way into Mom and Dad's dark room, went directly to Dad's side of the bed, and woke him up to confess my guilty conscience. I set the note on his bedside table and shoved the pink slip in his face as I blubbered my explanation about the day before through many tears and quivering lips. Dad listened with heavy blinking eyes while propped on his elbow. He nodded that he heard my words. When I finished my confession, Dad nodded one final time and flashed me a prideful smirk before letting out a long sigh as he laid back down and pulled the sheets over his shoulders again.

I stood there watching Dad find a comfortable place on his pillow. He was adjusting it here and there until he got it just right. He reached through the top of the sheet and wiped some sleep from his eyes. I waited. I felt so much lighter than when I had walked in. I was so thankful to have that burden off my chest. Still, I was fearful of the consequences of standing up against those boys. I began to feel that burden start to creep into my mind. But not for long.

Finally, Dad spoke. Blinking a couple of times and then wholly closing his eyes. With eyes shut Dad asked one question, "Is your friend, the girl, okay?" I answered, "Yes, Daddy. She just got some bruises and scratches." Eyes still closed, Dad made a single statement, *"Good job, Pal."* He brushed me out of his room with a flip of his hand from under the sheets.

When I turned and walked out of that bedroom, I was a free man with restored confidence. Instantly, I was again much more like the all-American, God-fearing kid who picked a fight with a bully to save a princess rather than the violent, pathetic, emasculated boy I believed myself to be since 3:30 p.m. the prior afternoon. Maybe I was wrong to meet violence with violence in protecting the girl I had a crush on. But my dad treated me as if I was in the right, I had been the hero, and he was proud of me. What a gift my dad gave me.

I didn't hear another thing about this event until almost thirty years later.

Beating Up Baddies Vol. 2

When I was in my late thirties, I learned from my mom that she and Dad had to talk to my teacher and the school principal about my aggressive behavior toward the kid I confronted. Somehow, my motivation for why I acted out and punched the school bully remained a nonissue to the school. They didn't seem to care about how those boys had treated all the others in the game, not to mention my friend who the boys had physically harmed. So on my behalf, Dad and Mom handled the mess I'd made. Voicing their displeasure with the school shielded me from ongoing residual hassling from my teacher and the playground ladies about the event. Dad and Mom did it quietly, never telling me of the meetings.

Believing I had done the right thing—the brave all-American, God-fearing thing—my parents willingly took the heat for my actions.

Diddly-Squat

I always thought I had known the end of that story. I believed I knew the entire context of the situation in full. Heck, I thought I had written the end of the story on my own. In truth, I had no idea how much of the story I was oblivious to, how much of the context I was missing. I had no idea important contextual events extended beyond that one Saturday morning on my dad's side of the bed when I confessed. I had no clue the dialogue went from the bedside back to my classroom and then into the principal's office for my parents.

As it was with my parents—who worked things out on my behalf in a much greater context to cover for me—it was much the same with my understanding of Jesus. Not knowing how to be heroic as Jesus was heroic handicapped me for years. *Not truly knowing Jesus made appreciating my design, made knowing my correct context, made finding my purpose darn near impossible.* I thought I knew the end of the story. It turns out that I knew only a tiny bit more than diddly squat.

Hero Duty Vol. 2

All-American, God-fearing heroes raised my dad. All-American, God-fearing heroes raised the heroes who raised my dad. Heroism was bred into Dad just as he bred and trained that heroism into me.

At least, that particular concept of hero or hero duty was bred into Dad and me. In those days, if families didn't foster all-American heroism, it could still have been caught and taught by neighbors, schools, church, and popular culture.

In any case, eventually, the quest Dad and I were both raised to complete was remapped by a divine cartographer—God the Father, the Great Storyteller—who instead led us both to a deep friendship and reliance on His Son, Jesus Christ, the Great Hero. Our personal relationships with Jesus guided us both away from the all-American, God-fearing destination we initially aimed for and into a heroism so, so much more necessary and fulfilling. Yes, we ultimately made it to true heroism; we got all the way there.

The only problem was, it would take us both decades.

GRITTY

Challenger

"The crew of the space shuttle Challenger honored us by the manner in which they lived their lives. We will never forget them, nor the last time we saw them, this morning, as they prepared for their journey and waved goodbye and 'slipped the surly bonds of Earth' to 'touch the face of God.'" —U.S. President Ronald Reagan

On January 28, 1986, I was nine and a half years old. That was the day I watched the Space Shuttle Challenger disaster coverage from home, not school. I had stayed home sick that day. Dad called me on the phone as soon as he heard the news, telling me what had happened and that he felt it was vital for me to watch the news:

"Scotter, something important has happened in our country. It's very sad. It might even scare you a little. But it's very heroic. I want you to watch the news. It's important. We'll talk and pray about it tonight. I love you."

All day long I stared at every hour of coverage from every anchor and commentator I could until my dad got home from work that night. I felt things were so out of control. There were countless guesses, but no one knew anything other than seven space shuttle crew members were dead. Until that day, I don't ever remember realizing heroes sometimes didn't stay alive to know they were ever considered a hero. There was a risk of spectacular, painful, or even deadly failure when taking the role of one of the first few people to do something potentially great.

While teachers all around the country had turned off the televisions to protect school children from the confusion and fear of the Challenger disaster, my dad called me from work to tell me precisely the opposite; to watch and pay attention when others were looking away. Dad didn't want me to close my eyes when I had the opportunity to learn something about honor, dignity, or patriotism. He wanted to teach me I might have to make the same sacrifice someday. Dad wanted me to know there was life on the other side of death, not to fear death. To be watchful, listen, be courageous, take action, and fall asleep every night with a peaceful mind, with my dignity intact.

This principle was one of the greatest gifts my dad ever gave me. It was his way of teaching me I had to be paying attention to know when to dive in and help others. If I was aware and looking, I could be one of those who bolted in when others were jumping out. I could be one of those who lived life by principle, not emotion.

And while I strove to be driven by principle like Dad, I *couldn't* be just like him. I was me. Emotion *would* eventually hijack weeks, months, and years of my life, not always but far too often.

This leads me to one of the most meaningful yet most difficult sentences to eliminate from my thinking and emotions as a young adult . . . and maybe even into my mid-thirties. *"The Boxes are Hosses."*

Hosses

"The Boxes are Hosses."

Dad would occasionally mention in passing, "Scotter, us Boxes, we're no dummies, though we'll never be the smartest. This means we need to pray for wisdom and work the hardest. The Boxes are Hosses!" I specifically remember Dad's younger brother, Uncle Jim, often shaking my hand and saying, "Scotter! You're a total Hoss!" I didn't know what the word meant other than its context made me feel like Hercules. The term "Hoss" made me think I was built and equipped to jump headfirst and survive anything. Honestly, when I think back, I still like the sound of it. Hoss. I still think of it fondly and consider it a powerful and meaningful (although, ultimately not helpful or exactly healthy) thing to have instilled into my mind and heart. Regardless, "The Boxes are Hosses" sure sounded cool.

For many years in American culture, the nickname "Hoss" represented the epitome of Wild West, cowboys and Indians, God-fearing, all-American heroism. Eventually, I found out "Hoss" referred to the fantastic character in the old hit American Western television show Bonanza. The show ran for fourteen years, and Eric "Hoss" Cartwright was the character at the heart of the show. Hoss was played by actor Dan Blocker, a gentle giant who had massive strength and would come through or often save the day for any family or friend. And in real life, Blocker was an actual gentle and caring person deeply loved by Hollywood and fans. Interestingly, Blocker played his character with a powerful quote from an old Quaker Missionary, Stephen Grellet, in mind:

> *"We shall pass this way on Earth, but once, if there is any kindness we can show or good act we can do, let us do it now, for we will never pass this way again."*

And that was what a Box man was to do—but on steroids—'cause the Boxes are Hosses.

It was a sad day for many fans when Dan Blocker died at forty-three years old of a pulmonary embolism after an emergency gallbladder surgery. In its thirteenth season, Bonanza had to limp to the finish line minus the show's genuine heart, "Hoss" Cartwright.

As time went on in my life, I began to limp figuratively because I had attached yet another emotionally potent heroic idea to my body. The "Boxes are Hosses" was just one of many heroic burdens I eventually heaved around; my "heroic Frankenstein" had grown a new appendage.

The Bulldog Vol. 1

Hero duty, mortality, and eternity collided for the first time in an extremely meaningful and long-term manner on another day in the spring of 1986.

One morning before lunch, Mom came home from a church Bible study with a standard paper-sized yellow envelope in hand. Offering me the delivery with a big grin and saying, "Now, open carefully," I opened the envelope quickly with great curiosity. Mom was beaming. I reached in and slowly removed a signed picture with handwriting scribbled across:

"To Scott, God bless. John 3:16." —Orel Hershiser

I lost my mind in excitement. I was ten years old, and *the* Orel Hershiser, the "Bulldog," knew about me! I know now this was a regular and straightforward thing professional athletes do, but back then, well, it felt extraordinary. What blew my mind was, I didn't just have Hershiser's signature; he had personalized it, "To Scott."

Orel Hershiser was a Major League Baseball player for the Los Angeles Dodgers. And learning I loved baseball, Orel's wife Jamie had given my mom the picture and signature as a gift that morning at the Bible study they attended together. It was a total surprise to me.

As families, the Hershisers and Boxes were two of hundreds and hundreds of young families who attended Pastor Chuck Swindoll's church, Evangelical Free, in Fullerton, California. Outside the Bible Study connection, we didn't know each other or hang out except on the occasional Sunday morning with thousands of others in attendance. I never saw the Hershisers in person.

In other words, I should have been a nobody to Mr. Hershiser. But I wasn't.

The thing is, there was something uniquely powerful about the otherwise insubstantial indirect interaction between Hershiser and me. That is, Orel Hershiser loved Jesus and told me about it. Not only that, he directed my attention away from himself. Hershiser pointed to the Great Hero, Jesus Christ, and eternity.

The Bulldog Vol. 2

"For God so loved the world that he gave his one and only Son, that whoever believes in him shall not perish but have eternal life."
—John 3:16

Let's be clear. I was a kid! John 3:16 was brand new to me. Heck opening my Bible to find any specific verse was brand new to me. If you only partially imagine the impact Hershiser's seven little scribbles had on me, you'll still be in the ballpark. They were eternal in nature. And it would be impossible for me to calculate their impact. It has been lifelong. The seeds of my belief and faith were given a deep drink of water. I didn't specifically know it at the time, but my mortality, my heroism, my worship, and my eternity all became metaphorical pieces of a puzzle dropped onto the same table in that one moment in time. That puzzle would be a dilemma I would work to solve for many years to come.

A divine moment of eternal genesis was extended into my heart by seven scribbled words.

Orel Hershiser and his wife weren't pastors or music leaders, and they didn't say a single word about hero or worship. All they did were two basic things: The Hershisers were *pursuing* their faith in Jesus as best as they knew how, and the Hershisers were *reflecting* their faith in Jesus as best as they knew how.

That's it. And these two things later became the fundamental basis for my understanding of Jesus' teaching of true worship and model of true heroism.

In the meantime, for the next eight years, I woke up and went to sleep looking at Orel and Jamie Hershiser's gift to me. I would repeat those scribbles and the words to the Bible verse, John 3:16, by memory almost daily. *"For God so loved the world . . ."*

When I was ten years old, I was no all-star. But the "Bulldog" helped me feel like one.

All-Star Vol. 1

Outside Orel and Jamie Hershiser's gift to me—a gift I treated like a trophy—Dad's real-life trophies represent, by far, one of the earliest and most memorable examples of when and how my original definition of heroic took shape.

Dad kept all his childhood trophies in storage in the attic. They were organized by year and sport, resting in a nice wooden box with a lid in a part of the attic directly under the pull cord of one of the attic's exposed lightbulbs. The lighting gave the lightly stained box an amber glow. And when the lid was removed, well, I might as well have been Indiana Jones. It was like I was carefully removing golden treasures from a pedestal in a dangerous cave guarded by a rainforest of animal terrors and native cannibalistic tribes; to me, Dad was the living king, and these trophies were his riches. I coveted those treasures.

As goofy as it sounds, I remember thinking I'd inherit Dad's trophies someday, family treasures to the last. Eventually—I thought to myself—when I added my collection of trophies to his, I'd show my kids proof of the heroic greatness of the Box family. It's funny, really funny to think about now, "Hear ye, hear ye! Behold your great-grandfather's twelve-year-old Little League Baseball all-star trophy. Children, here is the proof we were great and mighty men!" A young boy's delusion.

As I grew, Dad would show his trophies to me often. I would ask him to take me up to the attic so he could unwrap each one and show them to me in detail. I did this at least a couple of times a year until I was thirteen years old. But I also remember sneaking up into that attic space too. I would tiptoe up the ladder and crawl toward the wealth in that trophy box on my own. I was always too timid to turn the attic light over the box on when I was alone. Instead, I would carry individual trophies over to what little daylight came through the air vents under the roof's eaves to view the flaky metal placards.

Tommy Box. Giant killer. Dragon slayer. All-star. Master Hero . . . or something like that.

All-Star Vol. 2

The first meaningful trophy I was presented with as a boy was the Fullerton Little League Baseball Indians trophy I helped earn, during a season where my team went twenty-three wins to zero loses. I was twelve years old, just as my dad had been. I, too, made the all-star team my twelve-year-old year and earned a trophy for the experience. These instantly became my heroic treasures and a source of everyday personal pride. As such, I began my very own collection of trophies, just like my dad. I started my own golden box full of treasure and wealth. And I wanted the championship, all-star, and MVP trophies to fill the top of my entire dresser.

Eventually, they did. I expected myself to earn more trophies than Dad. And finally, they spilled over onto a shelf that lined the entire wall above my bed. Besides the trophies, my sports victories were even more remarkable than Dad's had been. I was on my heroic way.

I genuinely admired my dad for instilling within me a desire to pursue all-American, God-fearing, heroic things; frankly, I couldn't thank him enough for initiating the journey. But as time went on, I would struggle to unlearn many ideas and lousy thinking that worked itself into my version of heroism, my heroic Frankenstein.

I grew to have an infatuation with trophies. I grew to believe I was a superbhuman, a Hoss, and that I'd save the day many thousands of times for the rest of my life. I was a "Boy Scout," like my dad, who would lead others to safety. I would have an invisible hero badge on my chest. And I would strive to fill my trophy box with the same all-star trophies Dad had, then exceed his total by double, triple, or more.

It was game on.

KRYPTONITE

Kryptonite Vol. 1

The moment I started stockpiling trophies was the moment I started amassing pride.

Remember how Superman was only susceptible to one real danger? His one weakness was the crippling power of a particular fictional element, kryptonite—it was his Achilles' heel. In Superman stories, kryptonite came in a wide variety of colors, with their effects ranging from simply weakening Superman to temporarily mutating him or dividing his personality.

I wasn't Superman, but I suppose it was not all that surprising to learn my kryptonite took more than a single form, too. I was up against the fatal flaw of mankind, and I was blind to it: pride. This kryptonite was making me a victim and a villain, and I didn't want to be either of those.

During those years, my prideful weakness expressed itself in two primary versions: *parent/people pleasing* and *heroic fraud*.

First, my context for heroism had somehow become linked to people pleasing, specifically parent pleasing. Maybe I was born with it. Perhaps I wasn't. Either way, by the time I was a teenager, parent pleasing was baked in. Yep, pleasing Dad and Mom was my first layer of kryptonite. I hate even to admit it, because parent pleasing lasted well into my adult years.

It wasn't until after my wife, Kariann, and I were married that I became aware of my propensity to look to Mom and Dad for approval. Sadly, Kariann and I were not in a mature enough place to make substantial headway in disengaging my identity from Mom and Dad's assertion they were proud of me. I know it might seem laughable, but during that season of life, I still lived for the times my parents said "attaboy." Words of encouragement from Mom and Dad went a long way with me. I valued my parents' generous cheerleading and support above almost anything else. The profound truth was, like Superman, my kryptonite—the version rooted in prideful parent pleasing—was a hard thing to escape or remove. It would take me many years to eradicate from my life.

Kryptonite 1.1

Life would be hard to deal with if I didn't get props from Mom and Dad every so often. But what's ironic and what made parent pleasing especially clunky between my parents and me was the legitimate affirmation Dad would give me in particular. Every now and then, in a strategic way, Dad would say things like, "You're going to be a great man, Son." I mean, how could my head size—my ego—not grow the tiniest bit each time Dad encouraged me like that? But in a way, Dad's occasional compliment was a burden.

The burden was, I believed him. I believed I'd be great. I believed I'd be a hero.

Ugh, I know how crazy that sounds, mostly, and probably, to those who never had a Dad give them such a powerful gift of encouragement and belief. It was a massive, massive gift I didn't take for granted. All the same, it was what it was; I believed my dad, and my belief brought with it a burden to please, to hit it out of the park in everything I did.

In some ways, maybe it was supposed to work that way in the healthy natural exchange between a father and son. And yet, my context for heroic things went from just parent pleasing to becoming tied and knotted with my well-meaning, all-American, God-fearing heroic Frankenstein rather than slowly freeing me into manhood and independence. My response to Dad's encouragement chained me to anxiety and fear of failure. My heroic Frankenstein was real and took on a life of its own. The burden was real. But Mom and Dad didn't do it to me. I was doing it to myself. I had a jumbled context. And a jumbled context led to a twisted mindset about heroism. Ultimately, my mindset was a burden because I feared the potential crush of my parent's disapproval. I despised the perception of failure, and I dreaded becoming a loser. That was the twist—it was a fiendish and meaningless twist.

Kryptonite Vol. 2

From a context standpoint, I was effectively very, very wrong about my "blink and you'll miss it" story inside the great narrative of redemption written by God the Father, the Great Storyteller. What this means is, I thought I was far more valuable to the great story of redemption than I was.

I'll explain. The problem was, as I became less confident in my understanding of the heroic definition I had pieced together, my pride riddled me with a pang of anxious guilt. I could not consistently come through or save the day as I expected myself to. I was beginning to face real-world failure, and I didn't want to face my failure with any kind of honesty. If I'd failed at being the great "Boy Scout" or failed to win the first-place trophy or failed to become the number one all-star, I didn't want people to think my failures made me weak. I didn't want to be viewed as a victim or villain either—after all, I believed winners were heroes. I believed failure created losers. I didn't ever consider whether or not losers became villains . . .

I'm not sure why I didn't stop to think about what an actual villain became when he or she won, but certainly not a hero. Maybe villains who were victorious became supervillains. Sounded logical to me.

When failure began to occur in my life more often, I ignored my losses. But ignoring failure only caused anxiety to build around my expanding guilt. I remember being initially numb to the tension. Then when the awareness of my responsibility for not saving the day set in, nothing could stop the steamroller that was my second layer of prideful kryptonite, the beginning of my troubles with fear; the moment I started to believe I was a heroic fraud was the moment I began to feel more like a villain.

Kryptonite 2.1

This was the progression: I fought hard not to lose, but when I lost, I felt like a poser. I felt I was living the life of a conman. I felt I was a heroic fraud. Feeling like a fraud made me feel like a villain.

Irrational and unsustainable, my prideful people-pleasing habit and being a heroic fraud sucked the joy and peace of life from me regularly. As I grew into a teen, I began leading worship music for church groups. To a degree, this meant I was playing the role of a hero to people simply because I had a guitar and stood behind a microphone in front of them. I began striving for perfection in my musical and stage performance.

At this point, if heroism and worship weren't already connected in my life, leading music from a platform in front of a room full of people linked the activities of heroism and worship incontestably.

Yet, because I still struggled with anger or lust, for example, I believed I was a fake hero at best. I felt I was guilty of villainy at worst. The tension was enormous.

Hamster Wheel

I could not remove my infuriating imperfections. So, each time I hit that prideful heroic-fraud obstacle as the years progressed, out popped hellish anxiety and, later, fear. When anxiety and fear gripped me in church, I began to feel like a worship fraud. Somehow, personality-wise, I guess there were far too many irrationally emotional things riding on my sense of always coming through and saving the day or being a perfect performer with a perfectly pure heart and life.

I suppose I had a bit of a problem in retrospect . . . right. Strangely, I became a slave to an unhealthy stress-filled mental hamster wheel at a very young age.

No Fantasy

Fear became the bondage of my perpetual heroic peddling. As my life progressed from my teenage years into college, early marriage, and well into adulthood, I started to entertain ideas that I needed to be saved in a way I would have never imagined as a child. My needs were no fantasy.

Something was happening I could not explain in my life. It wasn't merely that I could not get what I wanted, or win the way I expected, although that was part of it. The real problem was I didn't know how to handle the sense of fear seemingly beginning to boil in and around me. All I wanted to do was to eliminate anxiety. The harder I tried, the stickier my fear became. The claustrophobia was awful as life became tighter and tighter and more anxious and more fearful.

I faced a deep sense of consistent defeat. The feeling never disappeared, but eventually, my sense of hope began to leak out and away from me. Then, my need for truth subsequently became immediate. In those days, I had no idea how it would play out, but *I needed God to transform the incomplete, mutated heroic beliefs of my childhood into the seeds of real heroic truth and correct context into my everyday life.* I needed Jesus Christ, the Great Hero, to bring order out of my chaos—and possible villainy!

And while the Great Storyteller, God the Father, was always at work, fear was what was about to drive me into a crazy and confusing upside-down world. My context was all messed up. It was fiction. Fear was going to test every heroic dimension of my mind, body, and spirit. I had no clue what was coming.

So, on the way to Jesus and true heroism, things got a bit, well, desperate. I didn't want to feel like a villain. I didn't want to live in fear, and I really did want to get to safety. But I had no clue how to get there. I needed Jesus Christ, the Great Hero, to lead me to good and safe places. I needed a hero to give me hope and save me from spiritual death.

FEAR

Man Up Vol. 1

The driving force in my determination to get to safety—to safe places—and to be a hopeful person was to man up. For years, my context for heroism and hero duty had almost everything to do with manning up.

As was often the case in heroic stories, in my account, there was a woman, a princess, who became the centerpiece of my obsession with manning up.

I officially met Kariann Marie Gillett in the George Fox University food service one night after baseball practice. As she introduced herself to me, I was so taken back by her radiant personality and beauty I almost dropped the tray of food and beverages I was carrying. No joke. For a fact, I did spill a little drink from each of my five glasses of either water, juice, and soda lining the tray above the plates of food I was about to eat. I couldn't explain it, but literally, my fingers went numb for a moment. I was slightly embarrassed by my clumsiness, but I didn't care so much about that as I cared to manage my extremely wide eyes . . . oh, and close my gaping jaw.

Meeting Kariann for the first time, I got lightheaded and felt crazy flutters in my stomach. I might have been having a minor stroke.

The story goes, I had made an honest mistake and dialed the wrong George Fox dorm room extension trying to reach a friend in his room one afternoon. Expecting a guy to answer, I was surprised when a female voice said, "Hello, this is Kariann." I instantly laughed out loud. George Fox is a Christian university with strict male/female floor hours students agree to honor; a girl in a boy's dorm outside "floor hours" would have been frowned on by most people. Of course, this one particular friend—I'll call him, Corey—would not only have the guts to have a girl in his room before or after hours, but he would tell her to answer the phone with outright blatant disregard. He would have thought it was funny. And it would be exactly something he would have done to push the limits as far as he could. But I was very wrong. This "Kariann" was sitting on her bed in her freshman dorm room, minding her own business when I called her by honest mistake.

Not aware of my mistake, I persisted—I wanted to know how much info Kariann would divulge about the rules she was helping Corey break. I'm sure I came across like a total creep, "So, do I know you? Kariann, is it?" I asked with a casual, interested verbal smile, unintentionally sounding quasi-perverted, I'm sure. Firing right back with a kind but very direct, "Uh, who are you?" was Kariann's response. I was getting a vibe I should either hang up or go ahead and keep digging to expose Corey. Why hang up? I wondered. Just dive in! So I played along and said, "I'm Scott Box. I'm calling for Corey. But you wouldn't know anything about Corey now, would you?" I snickered like a complete moron. "Actually, you're right, Scott. Who's Corey?" she said as a statement, not as a question. She had no idea who Corey was and was totally innocent of what I was implying. Nope, Kariann was not Corey's dorm mistress but she was also not above taking a moment to keep me guessing. "Besides, if your friend Corey was here with me, why would I dishonor myself by willingly admitting anything to you?" I snorted out an uncomfortable cough. Dang!

As Kariann was talking, I had run the numbers I had dialed on the phone keypad in my mind and realized I had switched the middle two numbers of Corey's extension. I leaned against the bed in my room, silent for a brief moment. Double dang! I had just made a total fool of myself with some innocent and clever girl I had never met.

Knowing I was caught, I figured I didn't have much to lose at that point. I decided I'd lean into my stupidity. So I answered, "Well, Kariann, now you not only know who I am, you've learned Scott Box is a big idiot. But I don't know anything about you . . ." I paused, realizing I was turning the encounter into a horrible pickup line. I stopped mid-sentence and started over, "Ah, listen, I'm genuinely sorry to have bothered you . . . um, Kariann." Like butter, she answered me, "No bother at all. I know who you are and will introduce myself the next time I see you."

If I wasn't flustered already, her confidence grabbed me even more so. I struggled to know what to say next, but I pulled it together long enough to reply, "Okay, cool. So, see you soon, Kariann. It'll be nice to meet you in person. Ah, and sorry for suggesting you were hanging out inappropriately with my friend, Corey." I laughed nervously. She let out a real, non-annoying laugh before I made one last offering, "You're obviously way too good for him." As if she had the script right in front of her, "You're probably right about that." We each said goodbye and hung up.

I remember setting the phone down on the receiver and thinking, Wow, that girl is whip-smart. On top of that, she just made me feel like I am campus royalty. I had no clue who she was, but I prayed right then and there this Kariann girl would be attractive . . . and single.

A Few Days Later

A few days later, when Kariann introduced herself to me—that time I almost dumped my dinner onto her feet—I recognized she was the exact girl I had specifically noticed from a distance hanging out with one of the tall-dark-and-handsome George Fox tennis players a month or so earlier in the late fall of my sophomore year. Two things hit me at once:

The unspoken athletic code of conduct between respectable athletes made her instantly off limits.

And being a fair-skinned redhead with massive baseball catcher thighs—grunt—I had no chance. Or so I thought.

So when I eventually realized I actually had a chance with Kariann, I took it. At that point in time, I was all about flexing my "heroic muscles" as best as I knew how. I had to win the girl after all!

I'm not saying I was wrong to try to win her heart the way I did. I'm so glad I did. I think it's supposed to work that way. Kariann's and my early love story was something I still see in my mind's eye as magical, an undeserved blessing from Jesus. But I also want to be clear about how my mind worked back then. Attraction, romance, and real love were always primary in our relationship. But I'm certain, in retrospect, Kariann was also a primary reason I strived so hard to man up in those days; to prove I was no fraud.

Man Up Vol. 2

There's no other way to explain it; Dad had taught me it was my duty to come through and save the day for Kariann. It was my responsibility to step up and man up. Dad raised me to adjust every heroic angle toward my eventual marriage relationship with my wife. If I were to take on the privilege of marriage, I would rise to every occasion and overcome any adversity. In much the same way as I had struggled with being a fraud (failures) in my heroism and worship, I was setting myself up for numerous challenges from before Kariann and I even made it to the threshold of our marriage. Unexpected twists and turns of all shapes and forms caught Kariann and me off guard almost immediately. Not all of them were grueling. A whole lot of them were.

As hard as things would become throughout our early years, as I tried to man up, Kariann and I have lived uncountable extraordinary moments and experienced ridiculous levels of abundant beauty from God the Father, the Great Storyteller. Here's a couple of the earliest examples.

Kariann and I were married when she was twenty, and I was twenty-two years old. We celebrated our rehearsal dinner with all our family on January 1, 1999, in an elegant private banquet room on the Hilton Hotel's top floor in Eugene, Oregon. I had accepted—heck, I welcomed—that this was the day I needed to man up. No sweat. Everything felt so safe at first glance.

My Grandpa, Billie Wilson Box Jr., shared a verse with all the family and close friends gathered together that night. Standing at the head of the long table, a distinguished and regal 6'6" man whose perfectly combed gray hair shimmered in the dimly lit ceiling lights, Grandpa lifted his sport coat off his chair, put it on, then reached for his Bible from the table in front of him. He cleared his throat while my Aunt Cathy politely dinged her glass with a fork to gather attention. Grandpa read:

"Children's children are a crown to the aged, and parents are the pride of their children." —Proverbs 17:6, NIV

Grandpa Box expressed his and my grandma's pride in me as their first grandchild. He explained this verse was meaningful to them because it affirmed what they had found to be true about being a grandfather and grandmother: their love for their grandchildren only increased with every successive child, never dividing into pieces. I was the first of eight grandchildren, and their love for me had never decreased. "Amazingly, somehow, our love for you, Scott, has even expanded," Grandpa exclaimed as he winked and grinned. He shared how he and Grandma thanked Jesus for having been blessed with the years to experience the expansion of their love for one another, for their kids, and their grandchildren. He told us how special it was for them to know their love had expanded outward to Kariann and her family, too. God's favor upon our family was enormous, Grandpa told us all.

Then Grandpa concluded, "Scott, you are our first grandchild. Grandma and I are proud of you. We love you. Love your wife the way Jesus has loved you, and together you'll have nothing to fear." Then he looked directly at Kariann. He paused, breathed deeply, and looked down at his Bible. Looking up, he smiled and continued, "Kariann, you are our first granddaughter-in-law. We love you. Love our first grandchild, Scott, with the love of Jesus, and together, you'll have nothing to fear. Kariann, you are as much a part of Ann's and my crown as any of our other grandchildren. We love you." Grandpa sat down.

I know I was still very immature in those moments. As Grandpa shared from his heart, I was doing my best to understand his wisdom. But this was probably all I initially got out of Grandpa's thoughtful presentation:

"God wanted Kariann and me to love each other. We didn't need to be anxious or worried."

Still, for some reason, I felt a little rattled inside. It was that very night I began to feel a new weight of responsibility I hadn't anticipated. I believed I'd accepted and fully appreciated the commitment I would take on as Kariann's husband. But I hadn't. I kind of felt a bit like a boy pretending to be a man.

Ironically, I wondered silently to myself that night, even with slight anxiety, how much more I needed to learn before I felt like a man. I didn't feel like one yet. I even questioned if I would be able to man up for whatever came next in Kariann's and my life together. I didn't know. I felt sick to my stomach.

After all the positives that night, I hate to admit that I was feeling a little more fearful than heroic. That was uncomfortable.

What I did know was, Kariann and I thought we understood what we were committing to each other. But we did not grasp the loftiness of it all. Maybe we didn't understand all the manning up it would take, the self-lessness, the sacrifice, the surrender—you know, true heroic love. But I'll define true heroism here in a little bit.

I know for a fact I had no clue the endurance I would need to battle the fear that would plague and push me into panic and desperate fight-or-flight moments in the coming years.

Becoming a man—or a hero—would not be as easy as simply manning up.

If only it had been so easy.

Firsts

I want to be clear: I was never more certain about anything in my life. I knew marriage was the right "next step" for Kariann and me. I knew what it meant on paper. I knew what it meant in concept. I had seen it play out in my parent's and her parent's lives in a successful way. I knew it would be hard. I knew we were young. I knew we had no money. But I believed Jesus would see us through and help us create a glorious life together as a new family. I just trusted. I believed. It was time to get married. I was 100% go for launch. So was Kariann.

No regrets then. No regrets today. None!

But first things first. The afternoon following our rehearsal dinner was January 2, 1999. The greatest day of my life.

Kariann was gorgeous, a beautiful and exquisite bride. The day was cloudy, and there was even a little misty drizzle in the air. Most of all, it was a day of sober vow making shared in front of and celebrated by over 400 of our family's friends and extended family. I was more nervous for that ceremony than anything in my entire life up until that point.

The wedding ceremony was held at Eugene's First Church of the Nazarene. Afterward, the reception and party were held down alongside the Willamette River in a massive conference room at the beautiful Valley River Inn. That day was a fabulous whirlwind of a day. Our families came around us to cheer us on and tell us they would support us and love us—with the love of Jesus—through anything we faced in the years ahead. We had a loving community around us. We always have.

Our vows meant something grand. And while I mentally knew what was at stake years before getting married, it wasn't until our rehearsal dinner and wedding day when the stakes sobered me serious. It was the first time a commitment I was making hit me that hard emotionally. Beyond that day of extraordinary joy and beautifully intense emotion, I had no idea the steamroller of fear I was about to hit head-on.

That first collision was only a few hours away.

Fear. Already?

January 3, 1999. The most fear-filled cab ride of my life.

The morning after our wedding, we dressed and took a taxi from the hotel to the small Eugene airport and boarded a plane destined for Portland, Oregon. With a layover in Portland and a long flight south, we landed just after dark in Cabo, Mexico. Our honeymoon was a generous wedding gift from one of Kariann's family members. That first day together had been outstanding. Just knowing we were finally married was kind of numbing, in a good way. But something happened to me on the way out of the Cabo airport that night. Interestingly, while being driven in the cab to our resort, it was the very first time in my life that I felt a sense of dark, panicky fear press into my mind—not quite terror, but more like dread.

Riding silently in that taxi as we headed out of the airport terminal lights and into the empty and dark countryside leading to the many resorts, full-on dreadful fear collided with me. I'd known fear in my life, but I'd never been hit that hard by it. I was a married man—the "old ball and chain"—sure! But nobody warned me this would be coming. Fear caused me to privately dread. "I am married to a woman who exceeds my dreams. Can I come through for her? Can I be the man I expect myself to be? Can I be the man she expects me to be?"

In the darkness, I felt a crushing burden of responsibility for the woman I loved who was sitting by my side, holding my hand. What on earth had we just done? We were two young kids playing like we were adults. Except we were adults. And both of us had only made the most significant commitment of our lifetimes: a commitment to each other. "Dear God, I made this official in front of everyone I care about!"

Our marriage had awakened a brand-new sense of awareness of not being in control. Heck, I wasn't even in control of where the cab driver was taking us! Could I protect Kariann if I needed to? Maybe not. The near terrorizing panic this caused in me was brand new. A new fear I had never expected had picked that exact moment to invade my life. A fearful responsibility I couldn't have understood until I felt its pressure in person. I was deeply scared of what I was feeling.

I can't do it, I thought to myself. I mean, I'll try, but if this guy pulls a gun or meets up with some buddies on the side of the road, I've got absolutely nothing to return fire with, literally and figuratively. I'm not ready for this. What were we thinking in coming to Mexico for our honeymoon anyway?

Maybe the worst and most lasting image I maintain in my heart about that cab ride was there was a tiny part of me, sitting next to my amazing new wife, struggling to fight off a deep sense of heartache. It hadn't hit me in any fashion until those tense moments. But what sledged its way into my mind was a real sense of sorrow. Somehow, I already knew in my heart I would *not* be able to become the man my wife thought she married. I was going to fail. I was going to disappoint her. Dear God, is this happening? I thought. She has no clue what she's in for. I have absolutely no idea how to be the man she wants or needs me to be. I'm a total fraud. Guilt. Sorrow. Shame. Fear.

It was then that it hit me, "*I am* the ball and chain." I was praying to God my collapse wouldn't begin right then and there at the point of our sketchy cab driver's pistol or something worse. I could think I was Iron Man all I wanted, but there was fear, and there was shame-filled grief.

I was never the same after that cab ride in Cabo.

White Knuckles Vol. 1

Who knows? Kariann's and my literal experience on the way out of our old life into our new one together that night may have been an early sign of my future struggle with mental instability. Then again, maybe it was just my selfish pride being "pinged." My context for my hero duty was still completely locked into pursuing my all-American, God-fearing heroic Frankenstein. So yes, I was totally selfish. But still, I don't know for certain what caused me to get yanked into such a fearful place.

One thing I do know for sure, what happened to me on that cab ride was the very first sign of the type of anxious, gripping, white-knuckle, dread-filled fear I would seek to make peace with and avoid altogether in the years ahead.

Fight or Flight

I was working for one of the most extraordinary bosses I've ever had, my good friend Sheri Philips in the alumni office at George Fox University (GFU) during 2001 and 2002. One of my wonderfully memorable and unique responsibilities was to assist Sheri in starting a student group connected to the alumni office to build long-term affinity with the school. Hilariously, that group was called the Student Alumni Council, or SAC—and every immature person like me got a giggle out of that.

One Saturday afternoon, a couple of the students I had the honor of working with, Drew and Meghan, came with me to a GFU Alumni Board meeting. In front of roughly thirty people, I stood up to introduce Drew and Meghan and briefly brag about them as the fantastic student leaders they were. As my time to make the introductions neared, well, it's hard to describe the sense of foreboding darkness that pressed down into my mind during those moments. It was a genuine agonizing dread, a fear not dissimilar to the fear I'd felt that first night in Cabo but even more pressing. This time it was unrelenting. I had never experienced a legitimate fight-or-flight situation in a moment like this before. But now I was, and I couldn't fight it off. It's not an exaggeration to say I was feeling the fear mentally and physiologically, probably even spiritually.

Unaware of my struggle, Sheri turned to me to proceed as we reached my part on the afternoon's agenda. I attempted to push my seat back and stand up, but I wobbled and almost fell back down into my seat. I steadied myself, but I was clumsy as I stood. I was not at all smooth. My knees felt as weak as I'm sure I looked. Even though I was standing, I could feel the tension in my thighs as if I was squatting to receive a pitch from a baseball pitcher as his catcher. My pulse was racing.

Anyone who has told you about how the walls close in on their vision when they were experiencing a panic attack—they're not wrong.

I fumbled and bumbled my words but thankfully had enough sense to pass the introductions to Drew and Meghan themselves bluntly. Remarkably, at that moment I had forgotten both their names. It would be like forgetting a person's name that you use fifty times a day every day of your life. Who forgets people's names like that? I sat down with a thud while Drew stared at me with a "Really, dude?" kind of face. My blank sweaty face gave it away—he and Meghan realized I was not playing around. They indeed were on their own.

Meghan jumped in to rescue me, "My name is Meghan . . ." and Drew piggybacked off her brilliantly. But I'd hung them out. I'd hung Sheri, my boss, out. Panic had taken hold.

It's still hard to explain the confusion panic causes. I'd fought as long as I could fight, but then I couldn't resist anymore.

Once Drew and Meghan had completed my presentation, the Board members clapped then looked at me as if I was supposed to say something else, which I was. The problem was I didn't remember where I was or who I was looking at in the first place. Thank God, Sheri jumped in to cover my butt and give the Board the report I had prepared for her earlier in the week. Everyone else covered for my total train wreck.

Weirdly, I remember smelling the sweet poppyseed dressing on the uneaten salad I had pushed out to the middle of the table too far for the servers to collect before the meeting started. As my episode was subsiding, that smell pulled me back into the moment again. I felt the drip of sweat running past my nose and down my cheek to the corner of my mouth. I felt my tongue involuntarily moving from corner to corner. It tasted salty. I wiped my face and stared absently, my wide eyes unfocused above the blurry faces across the table from me. Sweat continued to pour off my forehead down my face. I could feel the coolness of my collar around my neck. It was drenched. I loosened my tie, slid my butt forward, and my back slunk as deep as I could cram it in between the seat and the back of the chair. I didn't care what I looked like to everyone I had been so anxious to impress only minutes before. I couldn't fake it any longer. I had gone to battle and was beaten. I was laid bare and bleeding out on the battlefield. It was bad.

By the time the meeting took a midpoint break, the immediate terror had passed. I remember looking at Sheri, fully expecting her to be disappointed in me for what seemed to be a complete failure of competency in the heat of my duties, a total collapse. Instead, she looked at me with kind concern and nodded, "Hang in there."

Thankfully, mercifully, I walked into the George Fox University student government offices and laid down on the floor at the break. I had to pry my hands open; I'd had them clenched as tightly as I would had I been throwing punches. My knuckles were pure white. I threw out each of my arms to my sides. I sighed. Then I stared at the ceiling in self-pity.

It's not a relaxing experience to come face-to-face with a genuine sense of humiliation and wretchedness as a result of white-knuckled fight or flight.

White Knuckles Vol. 2

Leaving the meeting early, I went home to Kariann's and my house in Dundee, just a couple miles southwest of Newberg, Oregon, and the George Fox campus. I felt as if I didn't deserve her or anything I had. The panic attack wrecked me to my core. It did. My world turned upside down in a single afternoon.

Even though I couldn't control it when it happened, I was ashamed because it *did* happen. I had failed very publicly.

That afternoon with the George Fox University Alumni Board, I was out of control regardless of what I tried. There were literally and figuratively no bootstraps to grab hold of and yank me up. It was a free fall—it crushed my hope almost instantaneously as well.

For the next few years after that afternoon, without exaggeration, I battled with fight or flight nearly every day of my life. It was horrifying because it was so debilitating to my confidence. I had no safety net.

I might swim, or I might sink . . . I accomplished both regularly.

Depression

"Hostile accusers appear out of nowhere, they stand up and badger me. They pay me back misery for mercy, leaving my soul empty."
—*Psalm 35:11–12, MSG*

There's not much I can add to the understanding of the dreaded reality of depression so many people (even so many, many young people) experience in life. And I won't try to compare my depression with that of another person. For example, even a young man like the eventual King of Israel, King David, was bombarded with emotional darkness. He lived through circumstances I could never identify with. David was chased around the wilderness by the jealous and often madman-like King Saul. David wrote Psalms about the desperate, pitiful places he felt God was leaving him. And there was no way my circumstances or background allow me to parallel my depression to his.

But like anyone who has struggled with severe depression, I've had some profoundly threatening moments and bouts with dissatisfaction that have, like stairs, led me down into blackness. Those stairs eventually guided me into disappointment and, later, dropped me into the shadowlands of depression. Only a couple of times has my depression forced me to the edge of despair; it was usually fear that pushed me to that boundary.

And yet, maybe because of my absolute sure hope in Jesus, I have always believed I would get through my depressive periods. I have always had faith Jesus would pull me out of the darkness, up those stairs, and into the light again. Numerous events tested my hope enormously, but I never gave up on the hope Jesus would reach for me and find me.

So, while I've been in the dark times, I have always hung on for dear life, trusting the Great Hero, Jesus Christ, will come through and that He will overcome.

All that said, I've also had many nights where I have eaten an entire half-gallon of ice cream while in a depressed state—this search for food happened so often I gave it a name: "eating the kitchen."

Talk about kicking myself while I was already down. It can be such a terrible spiral. Funny, it was after one of those hour-long kitchen binges on a late Saturday night in early 2009 when I began to suspect I was lactose intolerant. Ugh! Only four or five hours later, the following Sunday morning, I needed to be at church to lead a team of musicians and a large congregation in worship music. I remember praying I wouldn't have to rush off the platform for the bathroom. And I almost did. I admit that's not the most traditional means of preparing to lead worship in a church.

In tandem with fear, and my deep concerns about being a fraud, depression caused me to wonder if I had what it took to be of any significance to anyone any longer. My all-American, God-fearing heroic Frankenstein was coming apart at the seams. I was constantly trying to stitch it all back together feverishly. Imagine that . . . that's kind of a gross thought, actually.

Depression can actually leave a trail of gore behind it, like a wood-chipp . . . errr . . . you get the idea.

Depression made me feel I had *no* moral authority as a worship pastor. I felt a shame similar to the shame I felt as a heroic fraud earlier in my teens and early adulthood, only worse. "How can I be as dark in my own mind and be of any use to God in the lives of others?" I would ask myself. I was becoming increasingly aware of my brokenness as it related to church work. I wasn't living in outright sin or rebellion, but it didn't matter—I couldn't make heads or tails of my feelings.

Eventually, I began to wonder if it was time for me to yield myself to accepting a line of work in the general marketplace and forgoing church or worship ministry completely. Oh, I tried that for a while too. I worked in insurance sales for four years. I was a good agent and very successful. The money was ridiculously amazing. And the people, my bosses and fellow agents, were some of the best people I've ever known. But I was never more unhealthy.

I felt I was damned if I did, damned if I didn't. Dammit.

Bootstraps

"Why do I keep doing what I don't want to do? I can't be
the hero. I can't be the worshiper. I'm so broken. Why the
hell can't I be the man!" —My journal, 2008

Here's a rhetorical thought I journaled only a couple of years ago as I
reflected on my struggles:

"Are there bootstraps in Heaven? Yes? Good. Maybe I'll
be able to use them then. In Heaven, the whole idea of
'bootstraps' is foolish anyway, I'm sure. But until then, in
this life, I can't seem to man up or propel my way through
much of anything. I live life embarrassed, like living with
my zipper down and all my junk exposed to the world. I
walk around with broken bootstraps hanging behind me,
like toilet paper stuck to my shoe."

Trashy and oafish, I know. Here's the thing; I couldn't eliminate the
ingrained and habitual idea I needed to pull myself up from the bootstraps.
That was my all-American, God-fearing hero duty at its most fundamental.
Whenever I saw people cutting loose old habits and addictions, I assumed
they were individually responsible for their spiritual victories. Were they
somehow more heroic than me? "Geez, maybe they are," I thought. I figured
they dutifully galvanized themselves into compliance and then success.

I never imagined, nor was I effectively taught, that I'd need Jesus to
make me an actual hero.

I didn't see the two things, hero or Jesus, being related in any way.
Well, maybe there was something heroic about Jesus dying on a cross and
rising from the dead and going to prepare eternity for me, but seriously,
they weren't linked in any meaningful way. I was dismissive, "Who had
time to think about stupid stuff like that?"

On the one hand, there was Jesus. On the other hand, my heroism. I assumed I was responsible for my heroism. Further, I never considered how necessary Jesus would be to developing true heroism. I saw Jesus and heroism as *separate and unrelated* things.

What it came down to was my context and perspective allowed me to believe I still had some ability to save the day for myself, to be my own hero. I could thrust myself back into stability any time I needed to—at least, I believed I was supposed to.

Bottom line: I needed to scrap the whole "bootstraps" idea. I should have. I didn't.

Explosion Vol. 1

I was immature, and my mind, body, and spirit were very sick. I even thought I knew how desperation felt. But I was not even close to being desperate for Jesus the way I needed to be.

The rubber hit the road for Kariann and me between the years I was twenty-six through thirty years old, between 2002 and 2006.

In 2005 our first child, Ainsley, was born. It was just prior to Ainsley's birth that I took on the exciting and promising work of selling insurance as an agent for the genuinely great insurance and financial services company, Country Financial. I worked successfully as an agent for four years. But for numerous related and unrelated reasons, those years were particularly hard on my health. Many converging realities were bottlenecking. As challenging as life had been—my professional work aside—it was these early years of parenthood where Kariann and I experienced a massive reality check. Everything had been tame compared to the expanding leak and later explosion of horrifying anxiety, fear, panic, and debilitating irritation that was about to occur.

Awkwardly, Kariann had to endure days of pure giddy goofiness leading up to the extended agitated state I would eventually find myself in.

It was so difficult for both of us to understand. And even though we didn't realize what was happening, Kariann did begin to recognize the pattern and would quietly be dismayed by the days that would follow either my emotional escalation or de-escalation. We became exhausted by the pace of life. The speed we were choosing to live was not sustainable. We had no margin before we hit the boundaries of health (margins are the areas around words in a book or a school paper you leave empty, so the words don't hit the edge of the document's extreme and absolute boundaries).

If my life had been a piece of paper, I was consistently hitting and exceeding those maximum boundaries. I lived life with no margin. I was dragging Kariann with me. And the results were panic attacks, back spasms, high blood pressure, and massive explosions of relational anger, just for starters.

Living life with no margin was bad news. Forcing something into a paper without margins created a giant, confusing mess. Another way of thinking about living life without a margin is how it's not much different from living in a house of cards—when one card fell, all the cards fell.

Explosion Vol. 2

For both Kariann and I, we were immature and slow on the uptake, but we weren't stupid. We were becoming aware of the onset and progression of my mind, body, and spirit's deteriorating nature. But because of my sickness—something we didn't know to label a "sickness" yet, much of life together was merely confusing. My deterioration was emotionally painful for both of us. It was real life, and real life was getting harder and harder to live. Confusion in real life was leading to fear about our future. The confusion was making hope a cloudy thing.

I began to gain weight, slowly at first. I weighed 215 pounds when we were married in 1999 to weighing 255 by the middle of 2005. From there, my weight ballooned. I ballooned and maybe even nearly popped.

By the end of 2005, I weighed just under a gigantic 300 pounds. Those last forty-plus pounds joined the party within the final five months of that year. Those pounds threw a rager of a party. I have the stretch marks to prove it. Nice.

As anyone might guess, new problems compounded ongoing issues. I started dealing with scary sleep apnea and disgusting acid reflux disorder. That didn't help my part-time worship music and song leading any.

I would sweat all day profusely, and my high blood pressure contributed to regular bouts of feeling punch-drunk due to my lightheadedness. I was a wreck. In almost every way, I was wrecked. *I wasn't truly heroic. I wasn't a true worshiper.* And even though I didn't want to be honest with myself, I knew it inside.

HYPOMANIA LAND

Cool. Calm. Collected.

The entire idea of being so messy and feeling so broken was an evolving vexation and disappointment throughout my twenties. But by age thirty, I'd lived over eight years with an ever-growing attachment to fear. I still dreamed big dreams, but honestly, my hope was depleting daily.

I was amazed; all it took for the Great Hero, Jesus Christ, to begin to save the day was to allow me to gain clarity in everything I risked if I *didn't* change. I faced uselessness/meaninglessness, victimhood/villainy, and hopelessness. So, when Kariann and I learned that I was a couple neurological chemicals shy of cool, calm, and collected, it made us sit up and pay close attention:

God gave me the same diagnosis the medical professionals did . . . That is to say, Kariann and I trusted God was guiding the professionals. Because He was.

Diagnose Me

The day my professional medical team, Elizabeth "Libbi" Hamilton, PhD, and Arvilla Claussen, RN PMHNP, told me they were diagnosing me with bipolar II disorder, I was overwhelmed with relief. To a great degree, the relief I felt was due to how this powerful medical partnership framed the information about bipolar II disorder and the future.

So, I should start with these professionals, Elizabeth and Arvilla. These two women were beyond credentialed professionals—though I refer to them casually by their first names, I do so by their preference and request more often than not. They were highly decorated medical professionals, but to Kariann, our children, and me, Arvilla and Libbi became members of our extended family. Still, my casual references to each of these incredible medical partners should not diminish the fact both Arvilla and Libbi were gigantically accomplished and respected authorities in the mental health field. They each had developed decades-long careers of clinical experience and massive amounts of past and ongoing education.

On top of that, Arvilla and Libbi were both women of intense spiritual commitment. I benefited most of all as a result of their friendship with Jesus. They were simply two of the most outstanding and most consistent representations of what I would label as selfless and obedient servants that I have ever known.

Sure, Arvilla and Libbi were not flawless people. But they were elite in what they did. And if it's not already clear, I have respected and even loved them; still do.

> "Libbi and Arvilla tell Kariann and me they are diagnosing me with a mood disorder called 'bipolar II disorder.' It has been a long time coming. And while rattling, it is also a relief in many significant ways. Most of all, it gives me context to all the mental wreckage and practical heartache I seem to be creating for myself and my family. Having

a definite diagnosis is, for me, a gift, not a death march. This puts so many things into a different context." —My journal, 2006

After leaving their office that afternoon, I remember cruising back toward our new house in Newberg, Oregon, the entire forty-five-minute drive home was full of relief and, "It makes so much sense now!" exclamations by both Kariann and me. We were exceptionally grateful to finally have an appropriate label to place on my "issues."

Bipolar Basics

Bipolar is a disorder with a spectrum of intensities; bipolar I is more intense than bipolar II. I should quickly explain bipolar II disorder at its most basic level, the way I experience it. This mood disorder causes me to fluctuate between emotional highs and emotional lows. Bipolar II disorder is caused by insufficient levels of chemicals in the brain called neurotransmitters. Maybe you've heard of chemicals like serotonin, dopamine, and epinephrine? These chemicals make a distinct impact on a person's ability to manage stress, anxiety, mood, sleep, appetite, memory, and even muscle movement, among other things. And the fluctuation of these chemicals can cause me to bounce high or drop deep emotionally. These variations can happen over hours, but they generally occur throughout periods of two to four days at peak intensity levels. At their most volatile, it seemed cycles would occur within even periods of twenty-four hours or even less. There were times where my elevated or depressed period lasted for many weeks at a time. In my case, after a period of feeling emotionally sunny and chirpy, I would almost always modulate to lower levels of emotional intensity over a couple days' time. It would function a bit like a period of recovery. Occasionally, the switch between one extreme and the other would feel instantaneous. It was so confusing. But as I became medicated, these episodes spaced out and became less pronounced in intensity.

Along the way I learned stress caused much of my fluctuation:

The less stress, the less change.

The more margin, the more balance.

The more consistency, the more stability.

At the beginning of my bipolar journey, Libbi and Arvilla suggested I was someplace in the middle of the bipolar spectrum, having had to manage clear instances of depression, debilitating irritation, hypomania, and identity-wrecking anxiety/panic attacks. They were correct. Their assessment gave me a few direct mental and even physiological cues to identify early on. A professional, practical, guided evaluation gave me ways to navigate specific experiences with careful focus and attention. Otherwise, I would have been overwhelmed.

One of the primary starting points was helping Kariann and me identify and adjust our tolerance to stress. For example, I want to someday write a book titled Arvilla-isms, filled with all the wisdom Arvilla Claussen has shared with me over the years. One day after checking my blood pressure and removing the cuff, Arvilla was turning around to store the equipment in its drawer when she offered, "Did you know you can lower the temperature of the stress in your life, Scott?" I looked at her with confusion. She clarified, "You have to remember where the heat comes from and who creates it. The greatest praise we can give our Lord Jesus Christ is to turn down the heat [of stress]. Scott, the Devil doesn't like it cold."

As if in stereo, Libbi would often say, "Scott, religiously avoid stress." There was a lot packed into the advice offered by Arvilla and Libbi, and without the full context of my bipolar journey it all might seem fairly simple. It wasn't. It took years for Kariann and me to adjust my/our tolerance level far away from the sickening levels of stress we used to *invite* into our lives. And honestly, before we could truly dial into a lower-level stress threshold, it took two or three cycles through the seasons of the year to recognize the various relationships, opportunities, or events in each season that threatened destabilization. During those times, it would often be one step forward, two steps back. But these pieces of wisdom were profoundly impactful in my quest for emotional, physical, and spiritual balance.

Arvilla and Libbi were very methodical in guiding Kariann and me through the quest for a healthy lifestyle. Still, there was a massive rush of new information and understanding to gather, process, and implement. But every session I received their counsel, it was as if the God the Father, the Great Storyteller, guided their hand to function like wipers wiping away snowflakes off a windshield. Sure, I've walked out of counseling sessions angry and unsettled with both Arvilla and Libbi, yet I have never left either of their offices without an action plan. They always took the time to met-aphorically take a cloth and wipe the windshield as well as wipe away the condensation from the inside of the windshield; I knew they had a system and a plan Kariann and I could follow to achieve health. I trusted them.

Seeking out wise, Godly, professional women like Arvilla and Libbi to diagnose me, draw a map, give direction, adjust the plan, and guide Kariann, the kids, and me through Hell was a little piece of Heaven.

This allowed me to find a great measure of peace. Up until that point, I was nearly powerless to the ever-increasing onslaught of dark, numb-ing moods that were countered by ecstatic creative, production-heavy days of bliss then followed by massive irritation and agitation. These early cycles before diagnosis and medication were rapid in their coming and going. Those times made my head spin. Bouncing high and dropping deep meant I could be one way in the morning and another by evening. It made Kariann's head spin, too.

Welcome to Hypomania Land!

"I wait for you, oh Lord; you will answer, oh Lord my God . . . Oh Lord, do not forsake me; be not far from me, oh my God. Come quickly to help me, oh Lord my Savior." —Psalm 38:21–22, NIV

In the early stages of my bipolar II disorder, there was a state of existence that resulted in living life for a period of time while feeling amazingly euphoric—it was called "hypomania." On the emotional scale between the most profound depression and most crazy mania, there was a hypomanic segment of emotional existence I could slide into from time to time. It existed in the artificial paradise below irritation and agitation. I suppose I could describe it as living an entire day—maybe an entire week or more—in the moment of excitement, anticipation, and glee of Christmas Eve or Christmas morning as an innocent child. It's hard to describe the joy of experiencing those childlike emotions as an adult who had hobbies and more mature dreams, and sophisticated capabilities; one thing was for sure, it was a giant, deceiving ego boost. In this hypomanic state, life not only felt good to me, but my brain felt very sharp. Early on, before diagnosis, and even after diagnosis, those were the times I felt the most creative and most happy I had ever been. Mild hypomania was not only a light burden—it was exalted.

When I was mildly hypomanic, I would become energized by options and opportunities and the availability of choices. There were times when I was not under external pressure to make a decision, so I would ironically test every alternative or eventuality before I would make a final call on what stinking "piece of candy" to buy. I didn't feel restricted. And it felt very, very good to feel so free.

Occasionally, I thought I didn't have to choose a single "piece of candy" at all. I seemingly felt I could sit down in that figurative candy aisle and pig out, trying it all. There were no limitations. If I was trying to learn about something, I could understand it all at once; or so I thought.

In these circumstances, time stopped around me, time blurred. In those moments, I felt I would be able to cram massive amounts of information into my head. I felt brilliant, and bionic at the same time. I felt like I was heroic again! It felt like the first time I walked through the gates of Disneyland over and over again. There was nothing off-limits, it was all for me. In other words, I felt I was capable of experiencing more, seeing more, doing more, or feeling things more deeply than anyone else. I could help people more because I was such an "expert." I was in my very own Hypomania Land.

I wasn't stupid, though. I knew the experience I was having would require me to leave the theme park eventually. All the same, I didn't want to leave Hypomania Land. So, my solution to something so slippery was easy: I would stop. *I wouldn't go.* I'd maneuver myself into a secluded spot and spend as much time as possible there. I would lock myself in place. Then I'd avoid direction and then detection. I'd stay in Hypomania Land as long as I could. When I was forced to leave—however, it worked chemically—this was when I lived the most intense moments of agitation. I acted like a kid, throwing a tantrum. I'd be outraged. I got angry. Really angry.

RAMPAGE

Illicit Drug

As much as I didn't want to go back to that demoralizing place of shame that followed the darkness of hypomanic guilt . . . who was I kidding? I did want to get back, not to shame, but my Hypomania Land. I was angry when I wasn't there, fearful I would never get back. In a way, I had become addicted to Hypomania Land.

Hypomania was a dangerous and addictive drug, illicit, in the deceptive sense. It called me back to it. As if on rails, chaos commanded me to circle back around for more hypomania, for more chaos. Hypomania was counterfeit health.

Bipolar chaos would invariably drop me into anger and fear. But at the time, I knew it wasn't something I could control. This was what was so disturbing; I'd tried and tried, yet discipline couldn't fix me. Something else was wrong. The seeds of anger and fear germinated within me, bringing to harvest a sense of guilt and shame which pushed me down, down, down:

I coveted the illicit drug I despised using.

I wanted to ride the ride I hated to ride.

I wanted to visit the land I hated to visit.

I longed to be in Hypomania Land regularly.

Splash Damage

"Another day in life, which way will I go?
Will I pick suicide? How will I say no?
The demons are calling me 'Just one more line.'
Voices echoing in my head these thoughts aren't mine."
—Brian "Head" Welch, Save Me from Myself

Save me from myself—yes, dear God, please!

Routinely getting "wasted" by the back and forth of a mental disorder like bipolar II was misery. It was slavery. It was also slavery living on the edge of panic as a result of fear. Living in that kind of mental, physical, and spiritual agony was torture I wouldn't wish upon anyone except all the evil villains in the world.

There was the initial and underlying deep darkness of living a life of unmanaged bipolar mood swings that allowed for, in my estimation, the slightest taste of death in life. Sure, hypomania felt like a bright spot. But hypomania only stayed shiny until I realized what *always* followed it.

After years of living with this disorder, I saw how despair could be a very legitimate landing zone for myself/people who go through the painful progression of disappointment, disillusionment, and depression over and over in life. If the ride down into darkness wasn't bad enough—the reckless coast into euphoria and the anxious, angry descent into darkness was rarely self-contained—the effects of my desperation leaked into the world. The leakage of anger and fear affected friends and family in all sorts of destructive ways.

For example, in this real life of sinful chaos, it wasn't like fear and love couldn't exist simultaneously. I didn't care what anyone told me about "perfect love casting out all fear." Yes, I believed that was God's promise, but God's promise was not yet my reality. I wasn't living a perfect existence.

In my unbalanced existence, fear and love unquestionably existed in me at the same time. I hated that reality, but it was true. And when fear was involved, where there was a leak, there was very often a splash. In a perfect world, it shouldn't be so, but in this world of sinful chaos, fear could dismiss love. Only perfect love casts out fear. Sigh.

It was true, splash damage could affect everyone in my life, even strangers. It's like the unintentional harm a bomb might cause to good things or innocent people after destroying the intended target. *Splash damage could affect everything and last indefinitely.*

My fear came from a deeply broken and chaotic place in me. It came from a need to be selfish. It came from pride, from my kryptonite. My kryptonite affected everything around me. *That* was splash damage.

I suppose that in a way, pain was designed to make people somewhat selfish, in part, to protect themselves from further harm. In my case, being in chronic mental pain tended to make me an enormously and entirely selfish person. Without relief, pain can—and does—lead millions upon millions of people into despair today. The effects of that kind of affliction, that kind of despairing splash damage, are far reaching. Terrible evil lingers very, very close to those people who exist in fearful desperation and all-consuming selfishness. Without hope, people die spiritually. Back to me—I knew Jesus, yes, but I was one of those slowly dying people.

I needed to be saved from myself. I still do, even today.

Out of Control

Life had been rough. Life with diagnosed bipolar II disorder hadn't made things instantly all better. Life was still super tricky for Kariann and me to navigate with each other. As it will always remain one of my primary objectives in life to be respectful and honoring of her, the thoughts and feelings expressed below are my own.

I was feeling out of control when I wrote this journal entry the spring before diagnosis:

"I can only imagine how Kariann grieves every day when she sees me come home from work. I know, shallow thing to say, but come on! I am physically out of control, and there is nothing she can do about it. I am mentally out of control, and she is helpless. I am spiritually just holding on. What good am I to her? I wonder if Kariann anguishes for what could have been between us, for who I could have been as a husband and as a man? What is wrong with me? Will I ever be able to meet *my* expectation to meet *her* expectations? Am I breaking her heart? God help me. Great Hero, save us!"

That Counseling Session Vol. 1

Given the words and thoughts within my journal entry from above, for instance, I guess the words Kariann and I were using in a counseling session sounded pretty extreme, maybe even a bit despairing, to Libbi.

I remember Libbi looked from me to Kariann, back to me, and asked us, "Do you want to stay married?" Her eyes were moving back and forth between the two of us. It wasn't a rhetorical question. She waited for an answer. She shocked me into sobriety. Once I realized the seriousness behind Libbi's question, I blurted out a desperate sounding, "Of course!" Kariann didn't let a second pass, "Yes," she answered.

Still though, I wilted into my seat. My head tipped back, and I breathed deep. Wow. I thought, were we really in a place we were needing to answer such a question? Were my "issues" causing us that much loss and grief? Had my all-American, God-fearing heroic Frankenstein let me down so badly? Yes. Yes. Yes.

Now, divorce would never be an option for Kariann and me, but, had Libbi not asked us that question, I guess I don't know. I'm not sure what path our subsequent choices would have eventually taken us. I know the choices I made as a sick man with an unmanaged mental disability were hazardous to our long-term relationship. There was no question about that. The road we were on *was* leading us somewhere bad.

So sure, I'd like to believe Kariann and I would have had another couple of opportunities to get things on the right track had we needed it, but it only took that one question from Libbi to rattle my head and heart back together. I had to step it up, but so did Kariann. Neither of us wanted our life together to continue along the path we had been traveling. And at that moment, I was willing to do almost anything to make sure Kariann and I would be okay in the long term. Heck, for seven years I blamed Kariann for nearly all our problems, from everything relating to communication to my frustrations about sex. And it was at this moment I changed. I was finally willing to honestly and purposefully work on what was wrong with me instead.

Right then and there, in Libbi's office, Kariann and I reminded ourselves what we had committed to each other from the beginning of our relationship. I said it out loud for the two of us, "Libbi, I know we're still pretty young. Kariann is twenty-six, and I'm twenty-nine. From the start, we have always wanted to grow up together." We had made sacred vows before God, family, and friends. We were not going to back out.

Kariann and I were committed to growing up and growing old together. We just needed Libbi to remind us.

Repulsive. Not Hopeful.

With absolute respect to Kariann, it would *not* be a stretch to think that I was a disappointment to my wife in some giant ways during this particular season of our lives together. That may or may not be true, but I was a giant, shameful disappointment to myself. My self-confidence was in the tank. I was a heroic fraud, and knowing this was hard for me to stomach.

I felt massive amounts of self-pity for the fact Kariann fell in love with me and not some other "less broken" guy. As much as I wished I wasn't experiencing this, I believed I was witnessing, in real time, Kariann's distress and lament. And in reality, I later found out, Kariann *was* mourning in her own way.

Kariann was an idealist—a good thing, mostly—but I believed I was the cause of the loss of her ideals. Kariann was absolutely faithful, but my insecurities were testing her constantly. As it was, she was anchored in place while my sickness was driving me further and further away from her. I repulsed myself.

Beautifully, Kariann never lost hope in God the Father's ability to restore the broken aspects in me and our marriage. She prayed and trusted and remained unendingly true. I cannot express my appreciation in words. She didn't need to, but she proved her steadfast love for me perpetually. It had to be exceedingly complex very often, but Kariann has always bubbled over in hopeful faithfulness. I'll put it another way, she's a hopeless optimist.

Then there was me. I was faithful, but I was a twisted mess of good intentions and heroic absurdity. And while I hadn't lost hope, I was not hopeful. Hope was still a thing I believed in, but it simply wasn't on my radar. It came down to the fact that I didn't know if I could ever overcome what I was enduring. Pain was causing me to see things very selfishly. Because of this, I didn't know if we could endure.

Most of all, and pitifully, I was anguished and regretful of all I had *not* been able to become as Kariann's hero.

That Counseling Session Vol. 2

It's hard to tell this next story without filling all the contextual gaps that led Kariann, Libbi, and me to this massive moment. So, I'm not going to try.

Every question Libbi asked and every statement she made fit the moment and the circumstances. Libbi guided us in a way that was necessary for Kariann and me to finally begin getting it as a married couple dealing with the extraordinary fallout and ongoing challenges of my mental disorder. It was a tricky puzzle she helped both Kariann and me build.

Libbi found ways to communicate and break through the stubbornness and dysfunction in both Kariann and me in a non-prerecorded fashion.

Funny, as I look back now, it was Libbi who represented what I came to understand as the greatest ingredient for heroism. She was a lovely servant to us. Libbi was Jesus to Kariann and me. She was a selfless and obedient servant.

One step further, Libbi was representing the Latin phrase *Illi servire est regnare,* or "To be His slave is to be a king." It was true. Learning how to define true heroism with a personal example of Jesus' love through another human was deeply moving. Libbi was a concrete portrayal of the royalty connected to slavery to Jesus.

After a tough week, Kariann and I were sitting together with Libbi in her office. That afternoon, Kariann had done more talking than usual and yet was still struggling to express her feelings verbally. As she fumbled about, I remember feeling incredibly defensive as she worked through her feelings. It was beyond frustrating.

I wasn't exhibiting my love for Kariann through patience. It was good Libbi was there to mediate.

I fidgeted and listened as Libbi guided Kariann with a couple of leading questions and statements. After a while, setting her notepad and pen in her lap, Libbi leaned forward toward Kariann and dropped this bomb, "Listen to me carefully, Kariann. I hope you will hear what I'm giving you permission to do right now." Libbi paused just a second as Kariann's eyes locked into hers, "It's just come to me you are mourning a loss and a big one at that. And I'm so, so sorry for your loss. Kariann, I want you to know, it's okay for you to grieve the loss of the man you thought you married." I choked out loud.

Ignoring me, Libbi continued while looking straight into Kariann's eyes. "Kariann, also, it's okay for you to grieve the hopes and dreams you were planning Scott and you would achieve together. It's very, very okay to grieve these very real things. All of this has mattered enormously to you." Libbi paused and thought for a moment. She looked at me. I was stunned backward in my chair. I realized I was crying.

Libbi wasn't wrong. She had said the obvious. I hadn't been wrong about what I was feeling about Kariann and me. Still, hearing the truth tore my heart out. Kariann and I were stuck. Without Libbi cutting right down to the real issue, we might not have survived.

It was true. Kariann was grieving what I could not be for her and our family. Her heart was aching with the loss of her ideal husband and all her plans for us. But what Libbi was saying was Kariann wasn't a bad person or some broken and shallow loser for feeling what she was feeling. And those feelings didn't mean Kariann had lost faith or abandoned hope either. It meant she was growing, maturing, and becoming more steadfast in her reliance on the Great Hero, Jesus Christ, in her life. This was basically what Libbi told Kariann.

One thing this event also revealed was that Kariann had no idea how to express her sorrow because she never gave herself permission to cross that necessary line for her health—our health. Libbi had now equipped Kariann to do just that. And I was there to experience the revelation. The hope it gave us both was staggering.

As Jesus had always been willing to do when speaking the truth, Libbi was bold enough to declare the honest truth for Kariann and me. Through her actions, Libbi had shown us how royalty or heroism in the Kingdom of Jesus Christ works. It's about lovely or selfless obedient service to one another to bring glory to God the Father, the Great Storyteller.

I was grateful. All the same, it was shocking. My all-American, God-fearing heroic Frankenstein was flipped upside down and kicked in the head in a single moment of time. Jesus and heroism had *finally* intersected at a crossroads I could recognize.

Through the Crossroads

This event was gigantic for Kariann and me. In a powerful way, it brought us both to the exact place of realization. We had reached a crossroads and realized we had made it there together. We were together. And that was awesome.

Yet to make it safely through the crossroads, we both needed to discover how idealistic, unrealistic—actually impossible—our definitions of heroic greatness or whatever fairy tales we had once believed were. They were toast. In my case, I had to begin to identify the well-meaning but distracting characteristics of my heroic Frankenstein. I had to identify the most deadly varieties of my prideful kryptonite. I needed both Libbi and Kariann to help me. I needed the Great Hero, Jesus Christ, to save me from myself and save the day—and dear God, save my marriage!

That day, Libbi showed Kariann and me to the other end of the intersection. She got us through the traffic safely. Not only that, Libbi had shown us that crossing that intersection, while still dangerous, could be done safely any time we needed to go back and clean up some of the garbage we'd left behind.

Kariann knew it. I knew it. Libbi knew it. Grief was a part of *getting through* the crossroads.

The Grief Card

Libbi made the strategic call to play the *grief card* that afternoon in her office. I didn't even know that card was in the deck.

And it worked. Both Kariann and I sat in silence, realizing we were going through the same thing, not different things. We were effectively operating on the same page and didn't even know it. Kariann was grieving. I was grieving. She was afraid. I was afraid.

In fear, Kariann and I were fighting against each other. In grief, we were drawing swords to exchange blows needlessly. It was chaos. Libbi was helping us realize our idea of marriage, in this case, was being challenged and refined by Jesus Christ. And Jesus' heroic purpose for us was what we were to focus on: to love Him by loving each other; to allow each other room to grieve while *not* grieving alone; to obediently serve Him by serving each other; and, for pity's sake, to stop being afraid. Order was coming out of the chaos. Hope was coming out of the fear.

Libbi had guided Kariann and me through the potentially deadly crossroads to safety. She reminded us we needed to keep loving each other selflessly. Libbi didn't say this exactly, but in my memory, I remember it as if she said, "Love each other with the love of Jesus, and together, you and Kariann have nothing to fear, *including your grief.*" I imagine Libbi's words as almost an echo of what my grandparents had told Kariann and me at our rehearsal dinner years prior. But Libbi wasn't done. On top of the grief card, she had one final card to play that afternoon.

Never Forget. Never Fear.

We had made it through the crossroads. Things were going to be okay.

But turning her head back to Kariann while lifting her hand in my direction, Libbi added, "But here's the deal, Kariann. This man, Scott Box, is the *actual* man you married, and he loves you. He's not some make-believe Ken doll. He's a real man. And he's got real gifts, just as he has real challenges. But you love him for all those things. You love this 'real' man. I know you do."

Libbi was talking in her relaxed sweet Southern accent, but the intensity was unmistakable. She continued while looking at Kariann still, "And you want to know something? In the years ahead, you'll face wild challenges together. And Kariann, speaking of together, you've got a whole life to live together. And I know you realize what this means—this means an entire lifetime of new and exciting plans to make that will thrill each of you. So go ahead and grieve what you've lost, but not for *too* long. It's time for you to expect Jesus will help you dream all sorts of new dreams for each other . . ."

Yes, that was exactly what Libbi said: " . . . It's time for you to *expect* Jesus will help you dream all sorts of *new dreams* for each other . . ."

Libbi readjusted in her seat and leaned toward the two of us, her hand still extended toward me, and said softly, "And Kariann, let me remind you of the context here. Scott is sick right now. It'll take time, but he's going to get healthy again. He's already making lots of very good progress. It will be hard work for the both of you, but Scott Box, your husband, is pursuing Jesus, and he is allowing Jesus to guide, direct, and give him the strength to manage his bipolar disorder in a healthy way."

Libbi dropped her hand back into her lap and looked back and forth between Kariann and me. Libbi said, "Never forget and never fear, Jesus is who makes Scott Box a real Hoss." Libbi looked at me and smiled knowingly.

That was the moment, and those were the words that solidified how I knew I had to reflect Jesus to be truly heroic with my life. Libbi's words galvanized my resolve to find a way to pursue and reflect Jesus the way she was doing. Slavery to Jesus was the example Libbi was setting. I was utterly stunned.

"To serve the Great Hero *is* to be truly heroic." A powerful example of what the quote "To be His slave is to be a king" meant.

Then, turning one last time to Kariann, Libbi added, "Kariann, Scott loves you and will make you happy." Kariann wiped tears from her eyes as she turned her head; her eyes met mine, and she smiled warmly. Then she looked back at Libbi. "I know," Kariann said. She looked back to me with twinkling red eyes and running eyeliner and nodded, "I know."

SICK MIND

Lying To Myself

Since 2006, with only a couple exceptions, I have become more balanced and disciplined in my management of my bipolar II disorder.

There was, however, one season in 2012 or 2013 when I had a "grass is greener" desire to try a different primary medication. I think I sold the idea to Kariann, Arvilla, and Libbi as "I'm hoping I can achieve even more emotional balance." I'll rephrase that. What I wanted was to feel closer to my memory of the good side of hypomania. Yep, I missed hypomania. Oh, how I missed it.

Now, I want to be very sensitive with this comparison, but I presume I might have been experiencing a mild form of what recovering alcoholics or recreational drug users call "relapsing" or, more plainly, "backsliding." I ached to get as close to Hypomania Land as possible. I wanted to do whatever I could to get there. The only difference was that I wasn't willing to fall entirely off the medication bandwagon.

See, after a few years of experiencing the benefits of medication, I didn't want to lose the balance it had brought to my depressive lows. I just wanted the highs again without the dark emotional slumps. And whereas

I wasn't using medicine to get to Hypomania Land in the past, I was now willing to keep my medication going yet try to *also* use it to get me back into the hypomanic theme park at the same time. I was unashamed about it too.

That sounds way more calculated than it was. What I'm saying is, I was lying to myself. All I was doing was cherry picking memories of the highs while avoiding remembering the lows. I wasn't content with the healthy balance of medications Arvilla had helped me establish. I presumed I could push things slightly higher without negative effects by altering my medication.

I Got Greedy.

Listen, I had been balanced for five or six years, and there was—there will forever be—a part of me that knows not to stop taking my medication. But after the time that had passed, I wondered—daydreamed—if maybe there might be a medication I could take that might get me closer to a perpetual euphoria. I mean, I suppose Arvilla could have prescribed me morphine if that was the goal. Needless to say, that wasn't Arvilla's goal, thank God, yet she was willing to entertain slight medication adjustments for my desires. But she was *trusting* me to be honest. She'd been down this road countless times before with others.

And while I know I was a mixed bag of emotions and motivations in that season, I fully admit, my intentions for a medication change were tainted by selfishness. And as she had been initially, Arvilla remained an incredible partner in the brutal journey I chose for myself. She warned me about the risks of side effects and complications of the various conventional medication options. I pridefully brushed them off. "Let's get started!" I exclaimed excitedly.

So, I tried a new medication, and I learned the hard way; don't get greedy. I got greedy.

Sick Mind. Sick Thoughts. Sick Actions.

After a month on the new medication, I began to experience side effects that put me in the most agitated state of my life.

The following three to four weeks became the worst suffering I'd ever experienced. Then those weeks were followed by another brutal month—closer to two months—of readjustment. I was adversely affected mentally, physically, emotionally, entirely. As such, those numerous months represented the only time in my life when I wanted to *fall asleep until it was all over.* That was the season when I learned to understand the unrelenting, suffering state of mind a person could enter when they made their final decision to end the torment they were living through by ending themselves.

Yes, ending my life would have been entirely selfish, but not in the way I understood "selfish" to be when I heard someone had committed suicide back when I was a kid. I now understood it from the other side. I understood the idea of suicide from the excruciating perspective of relentless pain. I could feel the slithering creep and crawl of claustrophobic fear threatening to chain me to unending, lifelong misery. Sure, that might be a selfish feeling, it was even irrational, but I could no longer lay judgement upon others after what I experienced.

A sick mind could create sick thoughts that could lead to sick actions.

I understood a little something of which I used to be ignorant and judgmental.

So now, to the agony of my medication change—it was the particular side effects. They included very scary things like choking on my tongue when I was eating and even when I was drinking water. I had crazy intense itching and other super uncomfortable skin problems. I would experience full-body twitches like ticks. My hands and feet would go cold and then eventually settle on the bitter edge of falling asleep and be numb for days. These agonizing symptoms lasted at least three weeks, probably longer.

Really, explanations like these seem so tame and don't even do the torture justice. On top of all that, the very worst side effect was the paranoia. I had never experienced paranoia before. So yeah, I experienced a relentless sense of generalized paranoia of all kinds during those weeks—a forty-day-long paranoia nightmare smack-dab in the middle of the transition.

I prayed so hard that the misery would be short. It was not.

Sure as Hell

During that medication experiment, maybe the one benefit of my all-American, God-fearing heroic Frankenstein was, even though I was in desolation, I fully believed my story wasn't going to end yet. I never wanted to end myself. Yes, I wanted to go to sleep until it was all over, but I sure as hell wasn't going to end it all! I was arrogant enough to believe I still had all sorts of hero duty remaining to accomplish.

In a way, I guess maybe it was my selfishness that pulled me out of that desert. As ironic as that sounds, it's probably true.

Look, I obviously believed in God. I believed in Jesus, and because of this, I never completely lost hope. In the end, as I reconsidered this event years later, it was the Great Hero, Jesus Christ, who guided me through the darkness despite my selfishness. All these years later, I realized I leaned hard on the Great Hero to rescue me. I leaned hard on His grace. His grace lifted me out of that wasteland.

So, yes, that three-month period and the acute weeks in the middle of it—all the miserable symptoms—were hard to describe effectively. The recovery took months, but it also offered me a new angle. Again, I was privy to one of Libbi's meaningful perspectives:

"Scott, you will know when the meds Arvilla has given you will start working. It will be like a switch will be thrown. The irritation will decrease, and you will know you are on the mend. We have designed a treatment

plan, and we will adjust or redesign it as necessary. And Scott, it *will* work."
—Elizabeth Hamilton, Ph.D., October 3, 2006

If you notice the date, Libbi had offered me this advice six or seven years earlier than the suffering I was experiencing with this medication change. I never appreciated her counsel the first go-around with my original medication, but this time I was finally in a place where I paid attention to the switch Libbi had mentioned. I had learned to trust her. And I found an enormous amount of comfort knowing I could believe her when she said, "It [the medication, plan, redesign, whatever] will work."

Knowing the switch *would* be flipped gave me hope when I felt closest to hopelessness.

Good Enough

Slowly weaning myself off that specific new medication and back to the original prescription was not an instantaneous or glorious thing. It was a slog. But then there was a moment one day when I knew the medication had flipped the switch, and it made me forever appreciate right where I was before the change.

The switch was flipped. I would *not* intentionally flip it again.

I recognized the trial and error involved in creating a medication cocktail that becomes therapeutic. Arvilla had worked hard with me to find that balance and then get it back. She was so patient with me when I called her in a panic while trying to be cool and not sound crazy. Oh, that was such a plague to be paranoid about losing her or that she might not trust me or, or, or . . . you name it, I probably thought it.

And that's when Arvilla said it. She said it in her calm, gripping hushed tone as she wrote me a prescription one afternoon in her office. She was looking down at the piece of paper as she spoke. Her words were a dart to the bullseye:

"It's not always easy to tell, but 'good enough' is good enough sometimes. I'm glad we found good enough again for you, Scott."

Speaking of good, I had it good. I just had a professional medical expert tell me "good enough" *was* good enough. And her passing statement of wisdom ended up allowing me to believe and accept that good enough was really, really good. We had achieved good enough once before, and Arvilla carefully helped me acquire good enough again. Good enough was so good! And finally, I knew it.

Getting greedy had been a big mistake. I made that mistake. Arvilla was implying a great lesson. She knew I had now seen the other side. She trusted I could learn to be very content and even thrive when the medication needle was pinned on good enough. She was right.

The experience of changing medication made me resolved to release my stupid, selfish daydreams of going back to Hypomania Land, that place of thrilling but selfish euphoria. I'd never be able to get back there for free—there would always be a cost no matter what. This situation proved to me the price I'd pay in trying to return to Hypomania Land was too great a price to pay.

The feeling of contentment flooded over me. I thank God I was able to find that good enough place again and be so serene about it. And when I did, I became inarguably committed to keeping it good.

When Libbi told me, " . . . and it *will* work," I believed her. When Arvilla told me "good enough" *was* good enough, I believed her. Good for me.

Oh, Stigma!

As for any stigma I held about bipolar disorder or mental disabilities in general, well, I hadn't had enough experience with anyone personally to have developed any negative stigma of my own towards those people. I was a pretty blank slate.

But as time went on for me, the stigma associated with mental disorders became more challenging. I began to consider maybe this was why people who didn't seem to care to know me might comfortably default to, "Watch out, Scott's a liability!" rather than, "Ooh, I would love to go get lunch with him to hear his story."

I got it. Stigmas were real. But whoop-de-freaking-do, what's new? Everyone experiences or holds stigmas in some way, shape, or form—everyone!

I used to have red hair on top of my head, a redhead. Today, I'm bald. But there was a stigma about redhead boys being irritating terrors who the Devil himself might possess. Eye roll. Whatever. I learned a long time ago that my red hair was not a blemish, but an opportunity to prove the stigma wrong. So, I tried . . . mostly.

In the same way, a bipolar disorder stigma was *not* a blemish. Bipolar II forced me to address things most people would eventually have to alter and manage as they age. I just had to adjust earlier than most. Bipolar disorder cracked the door for me to help others see things clearer. Bipolar disorder was *an opportunity.*

Bipolar II disorder became a crisis that gave God an opportunity to reveal what he could do to save me and make me more heroic like Him. Learning to be dedicated to my medication was part of that opportunity.

Dedication to Medication

I nurtured what I call a "dedication to medication" as a part of my opportunity—the biggest opportunity—to alter my lifestyle after diagnosis. I found balance and health in medication.

I realized almost immediately that I would do nearly anything at all to not become the sick person I had been again. If proper dedication to medication would help me never again have to endure the same type of calamity, *and* I was still able to keep the hero dream alive, then you bet your life I was willing to heartily embrace and accept prescription drugs for their role in keeping me balanced and healthy.

Metaphorically, the medication I started taking in 2006 was as much or more connected to doing or taking anything legal and prescribed by Arvilla to put the corpse of my all-American, God-fearing heroic Frankenstein back together—it's what I expected of myself, after all. I still believed it was my hero duty to identify my issues and drag myself along, even if I didn't feel like it.

But taking the "heroic" out of the equation for just a moment, this time, I didn't think I had to fight the battle for balance all alone anymore. I had a team, a great team that cared.

So, the trick for a professional medical team like Libbi and Arvilla was to work together with Kariann and me to introduce medication that would help me find a healthy baseline of stability with the proper prescriptions and then fine-tune the doses from there. The ultimate goal was not to eliminate, but to shrink or flatten the peaks and raise the valleys to achieve a much more manageable unpredictability level.

Thank God, my dedication to medication made the unpredictable, well, more predictable.

Never Fixed. Never Healed.

Altering my lifestyle and following a dedication to medication allowed me to achieve a massive measure of health over the years. My dedication to medication was my greatest opportunity, and I took it.

I was a man who had bipolar II disorder, and I learned it would be a severe mistake to believe I *was* fixed or healed. This, too, was a valuable opportunity.

The biggest mistake I could've made would have been to assume the medication I took to bring the chemicals in my brain into a healthy balance confined or restricted God. It would have been foolish to believe the medication I took removed His ability to actually restore my health. Foolish!

See, the thing was, I wasn't limiting God by saying, "I'll never be healed." What I was saying was "I'll never allow myself to believe, 'Wow. I feel so good. I'm all better now! I don't need to take my medication anymore.'" No! I knew what life was like on the other side of medication—or, on the other side of the wrong medication. Those were both terrible places for me. When I was in those nasty places, it was nasty times for those I loved.

On top of that, I had a good friend ping-pong through this exact medication nightmare for his bipolar I disorder. His loved ones were always left guessing. He could never settle the argument in his mind that "quality of life was better than quantity of life." In the end, he got neither when he took his own life during a non-medicated season. It was horrifying. His family loved him. He was a good, occasionally great, man. I want to be sensitive with how I say this, but because of his lack of dedication to medication, his family suffered deeply in his living just as they suffered in his death. I believe much of this suffering was related to my friend not being convinced he had a permanent need for medication. Oh, how I wish his story was different. I loved him deeply.

In the same way you and I need air, food, and water to survive, I always needed my medication to be healthy—and I still do! Jesus took the opportunity and used my *need* for medication to guide me to health successfully. My prescribed drugs were—and remain—the key to that success. It wasn't a concession to worldly ways either. Good grief, my dedication to medication was one of the fundamental pillars the Great Hero, Jesus Christ, used to alter the daily bad habits I was struggling to overcome in the first place, to alter my lifestyle—to make me more heroic as He is heroic.

No, I was not fixed or healed, but I was better. I was *way* better. Libbi and Arvilla were right. It took time and dedication—it took real trust and hope—but medication worked. My dedication to medication worked. And

I found that place that was good enough. I was not fixed. I was not healed. But I was healthy.

But for God's sake, the relief I gained from the medication also gave a little life back to the old heroic monster. My heroic Frankenstein was as hard to kill as a cockroach. Groan.

You Don't Heal. You Manage.

Since I was a child, I had believed winning made me heroic. I believed losing made me a heroic fraud, maybe even a villain. So how could I win and be a hero when I was in a battle with an unbeatable mental disorder? I was too broken, too sinful, too wrecked to win—this was the absolute truth.

Defeating bipolar II disorder was wishful thinking from the very beginning. It was never about winning. It couldn't be; that was Frankenstein's monster talking.

It didn't take long for Libbi to set me straight:

"You don't heal from bipolar disorder, Scott. You *manage* it. You will always need to manage it. For the rest of your life, you must manage it."

Libbi looked at me one afternoon after listening to me rant and rave about something for thirty or forty minutes. We had obviously talked back and forth a bit, but I had done most of the talking. I was struggling with connecting the dots between my faith in Jesus and the management of my weekly routine, and this was how Libbi nudged my thinking that day: "Your life is now, more than ever, about obedience. Obedience to Jesus *will* lead you to health."

I hope to never forget this advice Libbi gave me. It's a critical part of my story. It's also one of the great and wonderful ways God allowed my struggle with heroism to intersect with my desire to understand my mental disorder, my faith, and worship. The link between the pursuit of Jesus and the reflection of Jesus was continually getting tighter. Humble obedience *was* the coupling.

There would be many other dramatic moments ahead, but I could not overlook the blessing of Libbi's wisdom following my bipolar II disorder diagnosis. I had to circle back around to it many times over the years. Her advice about obedience made a gargantuan impact. It had been a theme. The theme had always been there. It had come up throughout many months of counseling. It was all throughout my notes. And I was only just realizing it:

" . . . The healing Jesus will bring into your life will come in how you choose to manage your sickness obediently." —Elizabeth Hamilton, Ph.D.

In context, what Libbi was saying was this: the new rules for living my life would not be about *healing* my heroic Frankenstein but about *disciplining* myself to hope, expect, and find rest in faithfully knowing and following, pursuing and reflecting Jesus—obediently.

Faithful obedience as a friend of Jesus became the primary prerequisite for my potential health of mind, body, and spirit.

My bipolar disorder forced my personal opinions and preferences about life—heroism and worship especially—not to matter anymore. Bipolar didn't care about my views. Bipolar didn't care about what I thought about it—it just was. Just like nature didn't shed a tear when it took a life "unjustly." Nature didn't give a rat's behind about justice. So, because these things were true, I needed to adjust, or I would continue to deal with the consequences of being stubborn.

While managing my health was occurring in steady increments, sadly, I still wasn't ready to live by Libbi's advice. I was slow to implement what Arvilla had also been encouraging me to do. It wasn't because I was a fool but because I was still learning, *and*, though mortally wounded, my heroic Frankenstein was still crazy strong.

Meanwhile, as this battle within me was raging, there was something else happening to me I couldn't account for. The more I would talk and sing, the worse my voice became—yes, my real voice. I had no explanation. What the f . . . ?

NO VOICE

Bull. Frog.

What the f . . . rog?

It wasn't just one thing like my dedication to medication that moved me closer to clarity about how to live an altered life. I wish it were so simple. I was about to learn true heroism and true worship were going to take a whole lot more than I initially expected they would. It was going to take nothing short of everything. It started with the loss of my voice—my real voice.

> "Jesus . . . It hurts to sing. It hurts to talk—a lot. I sound like a bullfrog. I'm worried. I think it goes beyond just allergies. It has to. This is a huge matter of prayer."
> —My journal, 2004

The year 2004 was the year I destroyed my vocal cords. For two years, I was afraid to seek help. Damn you, fear! So, I allowed it to become worse and worse before I tried to get help. By 2006, well, that was the year full of all sorts of bull . . . I mean, a year of sounding like a bullfrog. It was a year of getting yanked around by frustrating doctor visits.

For example, "Ah, it's only allergies," a doctor told me one late Fall. "Right . . .," I would think to myself, "There are tons of allergens in the air in *November through February* in the Pacific Northwest of the United States." Um, no, there are not. Idiot. But idiotic as the doctors might have seemed to me, I had no answers for them either. I hadn't considered the fact I had done something to my voice, that I was the one responsible.

> "It all feels like a cruel joke. My voice has hurt each day until today, only because I've tried hard to talk very little. But I don't know what to do with this. I have no desire to talk to people anymore. It hurts too much. God, what are you teaching me? I desire to allow you to finish the conversation . . . the sooner, the better." —My journal, 2007

My voice was my primary hero tool *and* my main worship tool. I loved to worship privately. I loved to lead worship publicly. If it's not clear, I lived and loved what I understood worship to mean at the time—playing music alone and for crowds of people in churches. And yet, my identity was being shaken down to the core view of myself. My mind and heart ached, "How could I accomplish my hero duty when my primary hero tool hurt to use and sounded like a bullfrog?"

I was in pain. I was fearful. I was lost—lost voice, lost heroism, lost love.

So, I need to talk about the loss of my "voice." Physically losing my voice was one thing. That alone was really, really scary. But the fear of also losing my voice figuratively was another thing entirely—we're talking a deep identity battle was raging inside me. I was dealing with the fear of losing my natural voice and my real influence. I was genuinely afraid of what was going to come next. I was fearful of losing what I thought made me my own person. So, I avoided addressing it as long as I could. I almost waited too long.

Feces. Fan.

I did not want to be broken! Broken repulsed me—it meant loser. Loser equated to heroic fraud. Heroic fraud equated to shame. And shame marshaled me into fear.

When I lost my voice, I began to move into a place of "Oh, God! The feces are hitting the fan . . ." The original version of this sentence used more dramatic and far less educated words. I was in this place of surrender because I was as mentally broken as I was spiritually. I was spiritually upside down, and I was physically wrecked; I had no voice, and I weighed 300 pounds. Fantastic.

It was when God took my voice away that I sat up straight. It was when God took my voice away, I began to allow God the Father, the Great Storyteller, to start telling me the real story and begin to reshape the *correct context* of my life.

"Uh, Jesus? Maybe a little help here?" I was pathetic. "Maybe you can tell me the real story, please? Will You help me understand the context of what is going on and how I fit?"

> "Talking is 'out.' Singing is totally out of the question, too. It all hurts. It hurts badly. Every night I feel like I've swallowed razor blades. Then every morning, I feel like I cough up those razor blades. It's unending." —My journal, 2007

> "Jesus, my throat hurts bad. Why is this injury substantial to my story? What do I need to learn from it? What is the point? I'm not vindictive. I'm confused. I miss singing so much. I miss talking without pain. What can I do? What will You do? Why is silence so important? What is it going to take to overcome this season?" —My journal, 2007

"I remembered also questioning, "God, if you're answering these questions, why can't I hear you?" It seemed like such a useless question."

It seemed like such a useless question.

Boiling

By the middle of March, the path forward had become clear: I needed surgery on my vocal cords. And I learned there was a slight possibility of losing my voice forever:

> "Scheduled my surgery for my vocal cord polyp/cyst removal. I have a right vocal cord hemorrhage caused by pushing my singing back in 2004 for the Creation Festival performance (it's discolored and freaky looking). I'm going in for the procedure on Tuesday. After that, I won't talk for ten to fourteen days. Intense speech therapy will follow . . . speech therapy. I feel I'm living in a nightmare."
> —My journal, 2007

After the surgery, I recorded my thoughts in my journal:

> "Surgery went well—it's been four 'interesting' days of quiet. Four days of not talking . . . dear God, nine more days to go. Help me!" —My journal, 2007

I have felt emotionally, relationally, and occupationally stunted the majority of my adult life; I may or may not actually be stunted, yet the feeling of being a man in arrested development has been with me for years. Living thirteen days after surgery without making a single sound with my voice was the icing on the cake.

I felt ridiculously defective. Now my "person" had no voice. At least, that's how I felt. It was a perfect storm of recognizing my defects had broken me mentally, physically, and spiritually; I'd been broken in every sense I believed mattered. And I ached for God to ease all the questions and pressure of my still recent bipolar II disorder diagnosis, the multiple layers of my voice issues, and all the uncomfortable problems of living life at almost

300 pounds. I wanted answers and fixes quickly. Why? My heroic ego had taken hits from all directions—oh, my pitiful pride, my kryptonite!

During the time I didn't speak for thirteen days, I had prayed numerous times God might speak to me. I somehow thought God the Father, the Great Storyteller, might choose those days of recovery after surgery to give me the script for the rest of my life. I assumed He'd go ahead and download the context for my life in my particular time frame, at *this* particular time. I suppose I was expecting some mighty spiritual data transfer from Heaven. Instead, nothing. Nothing! I thought I might drown in a pool of self-pity.

The good news was God did speak. The bad news was it took over a month for me to hear Him. It was a long time to hang out in that pitiful pool.

In these next stories, when I heard from God, it was like the Great Storyteller, God the Father, pulled me out of the pool of self-pity to give me the best butt kickings of my life. That's right, I got my butt kicked twice—both cheeks, if you will.

We Had Words Vol. 1

As May 2007 approached, my work at Oregon Health & Science University (OHSU) in speech therapy with my therapists, Julie and Lynn, had not yet provided growth, or really even relief, for that matter. There was a reason for this—me. I was the reason.

On this particular day, what was to follow was one of the cardinal moments of my entire life. While what happened was dramatic, it was pivotal because of what it did inside me, to change me. This event led to two butt kickings; the first kick to the first butt cheek was with words, while the second kick to the second butt cheek was, basically, with shoes. You'll see.

I'll start with Lynn. We had been meeting throughout April 2007 a couple of times a week. Lynn was excellent. It was easy for me to work with her. She and I spent time together at the beginning of each therapy session as she had to do two types of video scopes to document my healing progress. The first one required her to run a flexible tube with a tiny camera on the very tip up my nose and then turn the corner to drop down into my throat. It was an uncomfortable experience. But it was nothing compared to the other, more rigid scope Lynn had to run through my open mouth and into my throat while coaching me on how to overcome my gag reflex to view my vocal cords. I find it funny to think about all the gagging sounds coming out of that particular room at OHSU every time I visited. I'm sure it was a "business as usual thing" for the office staff, but it was embarrassing for me. Thankfully, Lynn was a great teammate.

Things with Julie were a lot more complicated.

We Had Words Vol. 2

Around the beginning of April 2007, after my second visit with Lynn, the speech therapist Julie and I were to sit down with each other. I walked quietly into her office. She was all business. Then, without chitchat or celebration, she began asking me questions. I nodded "Yes" or "No," and she looked at me, seemingly put off. I could tell she was all about efficiency—her time was valuable, and she was pushing me from the get-go to strengthen my voice. But I was sitting in front of her, completely quiet and confused, looking like a complete dope. I hadn't yet used my voice after surgery. She must not have known.

Literally, I hadn't talked for thirteen straight days before I first met her, having followed the post-surgery recommendations with absolute precision and more—minus a couple of surprise sneezes. So, when I walked into her office and Julie said, "Okay, say something," I flashed her an "Are you serious?" look; she must've thought I was acting sarcastic or difficult, or that I was playing dumb.

I don't know, but I felt my discipline of complete silence would be broken with a bit more fanfare than she was giving me. I guess I wanted fireworks and a cake. We got off on the wrong foot because our expectations of each other were a bit skewed—the hand-off between the doctor who did the surgery and Julie wasn't smooth. Oh, doctors.

Unfortunately, I spoke the first thing that came to my mind. I swallowed hard. Took a breath and said what I was thinking. What I said came out a lot louder than I expected: "Weather's nice today. Kind of gloomy in here, though."

Sarcasm and a voice! Wow. I was super impressed with myself. Julie, however, was not.

Next Four Words. Last Four Words.

Disappointingly, it happened like this almost every day Julie and I met. For weeks, we were both seemingly irritated with each other from the start of every session. Eventually, I figured Julie didn't like me because I was always armed to the teeth with frustrations, difficulties, and insecure sarcasm. On this one particular day, I could tell Julie couldn't figure me out. She was a speech therapist, after all, not a psychologist. She didn't want to hear about my thoughts on why I thought I wasn't making good progress. And I imagine my passion was coming across as petulant, entitled, and turd faced. The truth was, I respected Julie fantastically. But I was becoming less and less hopeful in a full recovery as each week of therapy passed without a minimization of my pain, chiefly. I still hurt when I talked. I'm sure my agitation was very apparent.

I'm also confident I was dealing with significant levels of depression-related apathy at the time. I imagine I had to look like I was aloof and possibly indifferent to Julie. That afternoon, agitated and a bit provoked by the friction I was creating with my "dynamic" language, I watched Julie suck in one of the sides of her lips while turning her rotating stool to look out the window of her office. Another something—something sarcastic—I'd said had peeved her, if you get my meaning.

As I continued to ramble, I remember the smack of her tongue as she turned from looking outside the window and down the OHSU hillside. Julie looked me straight in the eyes to shut me up. Cutting me off mid-sentence and with absolute earnestness, she asked me, "Do you want to heal, Scott? Do you have *any* idea what healing your voice is going to take?" She paused for a brief moment, "What's it going to take for you to get it?" I didn't budge. She didn't either. Then I gave a sarcastic lean forward—pursing my lips while raising my eyebrows, I dared her to continue. Silence. Julie studied me.

Throwing up my hands, I said, "I have no idea what it's going to take. That's your job, Julie!" She glared at me. And being a complete idiot, I felt like she was taunting me, so I continued, "And know this: there is too much at stake if I don't. More than you realize. Not only that, I'm tired of the constant pain and frustration. This is all so completely stup—!" Without letting me finish the last word, she was already sighing, "No, Scott, I actually *can* fathom there is a major portion of your future hanging in the balance right now. And I resent the fact you think I don't understand the actual losses you will experience if you don't get this right." Julie didn't hold back. I glanced down at her hands. They were resting with fake politeness in her lap. But I could tell she was feigning civility, pulling tightly on one of her thumbs with her other hand—with a death grip. I also made note she didn't say "we"—"if we don't get this right." Nope, Julie said, "if *you* don't."

Julie pushed her next words deep into my head, barely taking a breath. She unloaded, "So, you may have noticed, but, Scott, you are overweight, and being overweight, well, it's going to destroy your chances at a full recovery. You may not think I know what it's going to take for you to recover. But I know what it's going to take *exactly*." I looked at her with an " . . . And what is it going to take, All-Knowing One?" kind of look.

I was such an angry punk back then.

Instead, she ignored my snarky face. Without even a blink, she continued to verbally slap me, "If you decide to come back to see me ever again, you better come with all intentions of not wasting any more of my time." Now Julie was daring me, "So, your choice—come back, never come back. Either way, it's your life. The stakes are your stakes. It's your voice. It's your future."

She paused with her mouth slightly open. She looked up to the ceiling and nodded as if she'd made up her mind. I sat wide eyed and stunned, totally still. Julie continued, "One more thing. If you decide to come back, I have four words for you: *bring your running shoes.*" I waited for the punchline. Julie took a quick breath then said, "And Scott, I hope you're hearing me because these next four words could be the last four words I ever say to you. *Don't come without them.*" I almost instantly blurted out to mock her, "Wow, you are super good at counting your words, Big Bird." In that case, it was wise I didn't say what I was thinking.

Julie was steaming with pink-cheek intensity. Then, immediately spinning around in her chair, she grabbed a small pad of sticky notes and scribbled something on the top sheet of paper. She ripped off the note and folded it in half backward, the sticky top now clinging to the bottom. Rising from her seat, she moved to the door without a word. I could tell she was tense. But she was also still thinking.

Fuming.

I was fuming too. But I remained a mute statue. It may not seem as if she did, but Julie had my respect. I cared about what she thought of me. I figured I'd blown it. I'd never had a doctor walk out on me before. And as Julie stood at the door, I didn't want to show it, but I was pretty humiliated at that moment.

Standing with her back to me with her hand lingering on the doorknob, now seemingly resolved, Julie breathed deeply and jerked open the door. She stepped out, halted, then turned around, stretching out her arm and offering me the written-on piece of paper. She nodded at her hand as I stood to reach and take it from her. I didn't look down. I held her eyes, so she gave me a mostly polite half-smile, pivoted, and walked down the hall.

I don't know, but I'm pretty sure I was saying, "Sorry" with my eyes. It was the best I could do at the moment. I was thoroughly defeated. So, I didn't trust myself even to open my mouth to say, "Thank you" or "Goodbye." I had no words.

All my team sports experiences had taught me to offer a "Good game" to my opponent after a win or a loss. So it was a good thing I didn't impulsively and sarcastically honk out a literal "Good game!" to seal the deal. I realized any temptation to yell something stupid down the hall would be counterproductive to my rehab and . . . Christian witness. Thank God. I didn't want to destroy what remaining good grace there was between Julie and me—if there was any—with a knee-jerk response. I'm so glad God shoved a sock in my mouth on that occasion.

As I left the OHSU building, the small piece of paper Julie had given me went directly into my pocket. I wasn't even sort of fascinated by what the note might say—I may have even forgotten I had the note had it not been for the intensity of the final few minutes of that office visit that afternoon.

Julie's words, "Bring your running shoes" and "Don't come without them," were ping-ponging between my ears. I sheepishly plodded my 300-pound self to the receptionist's desk to sign out. Then I waddled out to the lobby like the sad, pathetic blob of a man I had become.

The Two Words

I checked out for the day and figuratively limped my wounded pride through the lobby to the elevator. Maybe I'd call to set up an appointment for the day after tomorrow, perhaps I wouldn't. I was entirely bummed and so frustrated. I was mad at myself for disappointing Julie. I was angry at myself for disappointing myself. The sticky note was where I had left it, in my left-hand pant pocket.

I shared the elevator with some other people on the ride down, so I waited until I got into my car to squeeze my hand into my pocket and pull out the folded sticky note. My curiosity had grown on the elevator's descent and my walk through the garage to my car. All of a sudden, I was itching to know what Julie had scribbled in those brief moments back in her office. I was about to be on the road for the next forty-five minutes or so heading home, so I wanted to know what she'd written before I left the hospital. I remember thinking, "If anything is resembling a cuss word on that paper, I am *never* coming back."

With the note in hand as I was starting to sit down into the car, I reached out in one motion with the same hand to close the car door. Then I accidentally dropped the piece of paper. As I reached to pick the paper up, a breeze blew the note underneath the car parked next to me. "Seriously?" I sighed. I was tempted to shut the door and drive off. Instead, I grumbled something I can't remember and heaved myself out of the car, only to have to get down onto my hands and knees to look for the note; it was now under the second car from me. And it was blowing around even more. Eventually, I awkwardly chased the small piece of paper down, finally having the chance to sit back down in my car, completely out of breath as I blinked at the yellowish paper. My eyes adjusted to the different lighting in the car.

In black ink, in almost perfect print, as if she had run it through a typewriter, I read the word—*Everything*. Confused, I flipped over the folded sticky note. On the other side, there was another word—*Takes*. Opening the message to see it in full, I could read it now from top to bottom: *Takes Everything*.

I propped my wrist onto the steering wheel as I held the paper in my hand. I let out an astonished sigh, "What the . . . !" This was no cuss-out, "You are a loser, Scott Box" note. It should have been, but instead, Julie had written an "I'm here for people who are determined to get healthy. You talk a big game, but you're all talk and no action. I only work with people who take action seriously," kind of message.

I turned the paper around in my fingers. It came to rest, stuck to my index finger. I reached past the steering wheel and placed the message onto the clear plastic screen covering the gauges and speedometer. I could feel adrenaline starting to rush through my body. Inspiration. Motivation. That note was an explosive catalyst inside me.

Takes Everything.

As I drove home in silence, I looked at that note over and over and over. I cried. I prayed. I thanked Jesus for His grace. I thanked Him for the journey I was on, even though it was so ridiculously hard for me at the moment. I thanked Him for Julie, who—seemingly—hated my guts enough to kick me in the butt in a way that ignited within me an appetite for something other than comfort food. I had just had one of the greatest moments of my life due to Julie getting ticked off at me.

Julie was right. To become a healthy man with a voice—a literally and figuratively strong voice—I knew I had no choice but to change.

If my only hope for health was going to take everything, I intended to give everything. So, I did.

To become healthy, I had to kill many bad habits. I had to give a lot of, well . . . everything. It was a lot to absorb and release all at the same time.

The first of these things that represented "Takes Everything" was to figuratively *stop* talking. In this case, I had to ironically start listening to and obeying Julie, my *speech* therapist. I had to start getting that right.

There was no question I believed there was too much at stake if I didn't change and begin to take charge of my life. I had told Julie as much. There was too much at stake if I let those few words, "Bring your running shoes" and "Don't come without them," be the actual last words Julie ever said to me.

Julie was no pastor or coach, and yet God had used her to get my attention, to rattle me out of the land of self-pity and self-loathing, to change me. To also get me to pay attention enough to obey Him *by* obeying Julie.

Too Late

"Takes everything" blew my mind. It gave me hope. I knew Julie had spoken the truth.

One of the most intensely frustrating aspects of life for me was the sobering reality that there came a time for many things when it could become too late to do anything about specific things. This was what happened in this case, something inside me knew this might be my last chance as a young man to not actually be too late to save my vocal cords. Julie's inspiration helped me come to terms with the reality that I didn't want to be too late with my voice or any other aspect of my health. I didn't want to be too late with Jesus either. With both of those things, I was right on the edge of a dangerous cliff.

In other words, I finally and clearly understood I could, in fact, run out of time to overcome or to change. Jesus, help me.

I was fearful Julie was right; this might be my last opportunity to overcome the damage I had done and heal my voice. In this case, this was a healthy kind of fear—I knew what was at stake, and I was scared sober. And thank God, I had a glimpse of the roadmap, what it would take, everything I would have to give. Evidently, it would take everything.

Yes, second chances are lovely, and life is full of them. Outside of marriage or having kids, this was maybe the first apparent time I knew in the moment that things could go *very* badly for specific and significant aspects of my future, so long as I didn't step up to the challenge. I had been given a second chance. And I did not want to miss the window of opportunity.

I didn't want to make the wrong decision, have that moment pass, and never be able to get it back. I may not have been a genius, but I had witnessed plenty of people let opportunities pass them by, only to regret it later. Not me. Not this time. Determinative things rested on my very next decision and that decision's follow-through; the difference was now, fear was not guiding my choice. *Hope* was leading me.

Bacon

My hope was rising despite my lingering fear. The Great Storyteller, God the Father, had guided me by helping me write one of the greatest episodes in my life. It was like He poured something fresh into my very being. And the best way I can describe that something fresh was, hope.

That hope did not come from some fluffy place within me. No, this time hope was hard fought—it would take everything I had. But in return, it would be wrapped in bacon by Jesus, the Great Hero . . .

I'm speaking figuratively, of course, but in less than two days, I would be desperately chasing that hope-filled "bacon" up and down the hills of OHSU in Portland, Oregon, in running shoes. Julie was pacing back and forth somewhere in the middle of the hill with a serious and stern look on her face and arms crossed. She would nod now and then when I trudged—I mean jogged—past and quietly speak, "Give me *everything* you got, Scott. Takes everything." In those first moments and days of regular exercising, I have to be honest; I was hoping the tortuous running of hills would end as soon as possible, but hey, a glimmer of hope was better than no hope!

Running those hills at OHSU a couple times a week with Julie's smug cheerleading was the second butt kick in the second butt cheek: out went desperation, in came hope . . . I suppose hope in any form, like bacon, was a good thing.

A Little Tune

I hated running. But almost with each step, real hope and the eternal correct context invaded my life as they had never before. I wasn't always aware of what was happening, but hope was filling my depleted batteries.

I was already different after only one run. Despite having to essentially lift my muffin-top belly off the pavement to keep my legs moving with Julie as my drill sergeant, it was like I had left winter behind for spring. No exaggeration, within one week, my voice strengthened to the point it didn't hurt to talk for the first time in years, and I had picked up my guitar to write some lyrics and hum a little tune. I ran every day. And I wasn't going to stop.

> "Sing! My voice is slowly on the way back. I took the chance to grab my guitar and play around with some lyrics I've recently written. Nothing inspirational . . . but hopeful! I'm overcoming my fear and my limitations. Really, Jesus, your grace is literally enough for me. Thank you. Thank you. Thank you!" —My journal, 2007

Changing the Rules

If it was going to take everything, I guess I had to give everything.

As I began to struggle with managing my bipolar symptoms—especially with weekly help from Libbi, Arvilla, and Kariann—we worked hard to get me to the point where I could start to understand and practice what Libbi would very often suggest: "How about you *give yourself permission to change the rules*, Scott . . . go ahead, give it a try."

What Libbi was guiding me into was a lifelong "safe house" of healthy habits. But as was so often the case with me, Libbi had to find a way to do it through a side entry or back door into my mind. Whatever those old rules were, I was a slave to them, and they were hovering around like stinky flatulence. I realized it would require a momentous shifting of the plates in my mind to permit myself to change the rules I was living. Something needed to shift to let those toxic gases escape . . .

My old rules, my all-American, God-fearing heroic Frankenstein, had essentially turned me away from actively pursuing, even needing Jesus.

My rules had driven me into pride. I was a believer in Jesus, I believed I was saved for eternity. But my monstrous rules had only gotten me halfway in my pursuit of Jesus. And being halfway to Jesus meant I was only halfway to true heroism. But in my mind, I pridefully still didn't see it that way. In my mind, I was operating with the traditional all-American, God-fearing, white-knuckle set of rules. The two primary pillars for these rules were:

I didn't need more of Jesus.

I only needed more of myself.

I was only halfway to Jesus.

Now, don't get me wrong. I feared God enough to have Him prominently displayed on my "trophy shelf" to take pride in, occasionally be inspired by, and for others to see. But living with heroic Frankenstein-like rules left Jesus out of the game and on the bench. Living in a world with heroic rules like mine meant all the good I hoped to accomplish heroically would ultimately be meaningless because Jesus *wasn't* involved. When I say, "halfway to Jesus," I mean it. I was a Christian, but I was not pursuing and reflecting Jesus as a habit. My Christian faith was only a label. The rules of my life needed to change.

> "Lord, speak. Lord, bring health. Lord, change me . . . God,
> I pray for your power to change the rules I have believed
> I needed to follow. Teach me how to worship You truly."
> —My journal, 2006

When I think back on my childhood, there was one particular morning I remember when the rules changed, even briefly. I share this story because it was a specific event in my life that gave credibility to Libbi's encouragement to "give yourself permission to change the rules." Having experienced the following story as a kid allowed me to broaden my perspective even years later as an adult.

. . . But first, the story about a song and an earthquake.

SWAGGER

In the Air Tonight Vol. 1

On October 1, 1987, I was in my room upstairs in our family's home in Fullerton, California. My sister, Mandy, and I were only a couple minutes away from heading out the front door to walk around the block to Sunset Lane Elementary together as we usually did. That particular morning, I was squeezing in one more song before we left for the school day. I loved listening to music every morning before classes started. So, I was sitting on my bed with my elbows on my knees and my head limp. Leaning forward, perfectly positioned between the two speakers of my cool black Magnavox stereo and tape deck, I had my eyes closed while playing the Phil Collins album, Face Value. I was listening to the song "In the Air Tonight." Sometime during that song at 7:42 a.m., the 5.9 Whittier Narrows earthquake hit the region.

Our house was less than thirty miles from the epicenter. And that earthquake was different from other earthquakes I had felt. It was radically violent. It was not like the occasional rolling earthquakes we would sometimes get. This one was different—it was called a blind thrust earthquake, and a 5.9 blind thrust was considered even more dangerous to urban or suburban areas than a 7.0–8.0 earthquake. The house felt like it was jumping side to side and up and down all at the same time. The chandelier over the stairs was jingling like a wind chime in a gust of wind. My sister's scream was probably heard worldwide.

In the Air Tonight Vol. 2

During earthquakes, our family would meet downstairs under the door-frame between our dining room and family room. But Dad had already left for work that morning. On this morning, my sister, Mandy, had been the first to the meeting spot. So, at eleven years old, I found myself loudly instructing my brother, Brad, and mom like a drill sergeant, "Let's go. Let's go. Let's go!" as I used the handrail to steady myself to descend while skipping multiple stairs at a time. I remember looking up, hoping the chandelier wouldn't land on my head as I ran under it. I hit the floor at the bottom of the stairs, skidded, and turned the corner to run down the hall and gather in the large doorway between the family room, dining room, and kitchen.

It was a brief occasion where the rules had changed, if only for a moment—I was the man of the house. I could tell Mom was scared as the house reverberated with not only movement but noise, like change in a pop can. Frankly, with respect, Mom was one of those who expressed a bit of high theater whenever an earthquake hit. Playing things emotionally cool was *not* her manner of operation. And while Mandy was typically less hysterical than Mom in those events, you wouldn't have known it based on the sheer volume of her perpetual screams of terror. Even as a young boy, Mom's theatrics and Mandy's hoopla during earthquakes were motivating things for me to try to overcome.

Making things even more intense in those seconds were the jars of canned goods falling off their stand above the fireplace only a few feet behind us. Each crash made Mandy, Brad, Mom, and me flinch and grimace as if the house was going to fall on us flat. Between Mandy's screams and Mom's short prayers consisting of only "Oh God, Oh God, Oh God," I remember repeating the words I had heard Dad say a couple of times before in the middle of the night as we met in the same place, "We're good. We're good. Our house is strong, real strong."

I was striving to be the heroic voice of reason and calm. I expected it of myself. But as soon as the violent ride was over, I wanted Dad to get home as quickly as possible. The quake had scared me like crazy, too.

In the Air Tonight Vol. 3

Upon returning to our house after the earthquake, Dad hugged Mom and each of us kids. I was massively relieved to have made it through the earthquake, as well as the fact that I'd no longer need to deal with any residual freak-outs from my mom or sister—Dad was home, that was *his* job now. Truth was, Dad's presence gave all of us massive peace. Dad was a magician with the ability to provide perspective. It was part of his love language, if you will. My whole life, I was witness to how my dad listened. He watched. When it was wise, he spoke. His presence was just calming. I learned a lot from how Dad handled moments of intense pressure my entire life. It was during those times I also imagined the invisible hero badge on Dad's chest made him proud too. I wanted to experience that same kind of pride in myself. I wanted to be a hero like Dad was a hero.

Later that day, after school, I went back into my room to listen to more music. Interestingly, as the first jolt of the earthquake had pulled me from my music coma earlier in the morning, I must have caught my foot on the power cord, ripping it from the socket. The cord was dropped down the bedside and in front of the table. It was stretching out a couple of feet with its two prongs facing me as I came in the bedroom door. I bent over, grabbed the end of the cord, straightened out one of the bent prongs, and leaned over the table to plug the Magnavox boom box back in. Because of the unorthodox manner of killing the power that morning, the play button hadn't been toggled off and remained compressed.

So, there I was bent over, pressing the power cord back into the wall socket with my ear only an inch or two from one of the speakers when the music started as if it had never stopped, from the exact place it had been as the earthquake hit. It was loud and unexpected. I hit my head on the headboard of my bed as I nearly jumped out of my skin—playing was the drum fill in the song "In the Air Tonight," and it almost scored a technical knockout on me.

That song and that day cannot be separated in my mind. That song provided the soundtrack to the adventure, the responsibility, and later the sense of confident affection Dad and Mom had extended to me that day. Hearing that song reminds me of a brief point in time where the rules of our family changed, for just a few short minutes, until Dad got home to take charge. I was still young, but it was one of a string of events that represented a season of growth from boyhood to manhood—to "hero." My own imaginary, prideful, heroic badge was taking form.

Deputy

But truthfully, the song "In the Air Tonight" gave me a warm reminder of Dad's steady hand on my back after he hugged us all that morning. He physically guided me to stand next to him as he addressed the rest of the family. Whether he did it consciously or not, Dad included me as the protector I had been in his absence by just allowing me to stand alongside him as if I was his deputy. It made me all the more proud of the fact I had been paying attention during those handfuls of other times we'd been awakened in the middle of the night and went through similar events. I had watched and tried to mimic Dad's calm but authoritative behavior. Funny, I felt like I had passed some type of "you're on your way to being a hero now" test. It was subtle, but it was meaningful. And it wasn't just assumed—there was something *very* real about it.

Later that night, Dad came and sat on my bed and thanked me for keeping my cool when the walls were rattling all around Mom, Mandy, Brad, and me that morning. Mom had told him how thankful she was. She was appreciative I was there, saying the same words Dad would have said with just the same balanced confidence.

The way Dad thanked me as an eleven-year-old kid made me feel I had graduated to big-boy pants. For a young boy, Mom's endorsement and Dad's appreciation was a tectonic event for me. The rules really were changing as my hero badge was growing. This was a big, big deal. It boosted my confidence and made me feel Dad had handed me an official sheriff deputy badge. My heroic jurisdiction increased exceedingly.

In my young Disney-like, romantic, Wild West imagination, it felt like real-life cowboys and Indians kind of stuff. It was all-American, God-fearing, and "heroic" to the core.

And obviously, I accepted my sheriff deputy badge without hesitation.

Heroic Like Him

I remember a time as an even younger boy, when Dad and I would play a game of keep-away with a racquetball while wrestling on our family room floor. Occasionally, my younger sister and brother would get in on the fun and create all sorts of enjoyable distractions and havoc for Dad while I terrorized his hands by prying one finger off the ball at a time. It was a fun, rough-and-tumble game that usually ended without tears . . .

Eventually, I grew too big and strong for that game. I don't remember playing it with Dad beyond my eighth or ninth year. I guess I could say the game ultimately was no longer, um, safe for Dad's fingers. I mean, I knew I could maybe break Dad's pinky finger if I wanted to by giving it a massive twist. But I always knew Dad could have squished me like a bug if he had desired in retaliation. It's a fact, getting the racquetball from Dad was nothing short of impossible unless he wanted to share the ball with me to give me the victory.

My potential for victory in that game was purely my dad's grace.

Let me be unambiguous: I learned from a silly kid game of keep-away that genuine and true heroism—the real spiritual kind—rested in the same realm of impossibility as getting that racquetball from my dad [I'm not talking about my belief in Jesus. I'm talking about *becoming* like Jesus].

Now translate this to being heroic as Jesus is heroic. Think about it; becoming heroic *like* Jesus was in the same orbit as being capable of jumping from Redmond, Oregon, to the rock formerly classified as a planet, Pluto—with only a running start. Being heroic as Jesus is heroic was as *impossible* as throwing a stone from the earth's surface onto the moon's surface with only my arm. There was no chance my jump or the rock thrown into the sky would escape gravity's hold on it. Ever.

There was *no* chance this broken man—Scott Wilson Box—could ever be heroic as Jesus is heroic. Ever.

Yet Jesus and His apostles taught I was not just to believe in Jesus, I *was* to be like Jesus. I was supposed to become like Him. Jesus was supposed to transform me into someone new, someone who acted like, loved like, and served like Him. Honestly? But that was impossible and irrational. I couldn't accomplish the impossible. Being a person who became heroic like Jesus was ludicrous. And yet the Holy Bible was clear:

"Whoever claims to live in Him must live as Jesus did."
—*1 John 2:6, NIV*

"Indeed, I have been crucified with Christ. My ego is no longer central. It is no longer important that I appear righteous before you or have your good opinion, and I am no longer driven to impress God. Christ lives in me. The life

you see me living is not 'mine,' but it is lived by faith in the Son of God, who loved me and gave himself for me." —Galatians 2:19–20, MSG

" . . . And then take on an entirely new way of life—a God-fashioned life, a life renewed from the inside and working itself into your conduct as God accurately reproduces his character in you." —Ephesians 4:24, MSG

"Beloved, now we are children of God . . . and everyone who has this hope fixed on Him purifies himself, just as He is pure." —1 John 3:2–3, NKJV

So, I faced a paradox. I *had* to set out to achieve the irrational. I *had* to choose to live the impossible. I *had* to strive to be heroic as Jesus is heroic.

Just as it was impossible to get the ball from Dad in one sense, it was possible—guaranteed—my dad's mercy would toss me a win or two now and then in keep-away. In the same way, I had to rely on the prerogative of Jesus Christ, the Great Hero, for my victory and my heroic status in this lifetime of wild, adventurous wrestling with sinful chaos. My salvation was settled. But here's what becoming a true hero came down to:

I didn't need my pretend sheriff deputy badge, I needed the Great Hero to toss me an untarnished heroic deputy's badge.

Heroic Swagger Vol. 1

Here's how Jesus tossed me the heroic deputy badge. Many years later, when I was reading in the Book of John in the New Testament of the Holy Bible, I read a couple of phrases Jesus said:

"This is my commandment: Love each other in the same way I have loved you. There is no greater love than to lay down one's life for one's friends." —John 15:12–13, NLT

When I read these words, I had to pause. Every word in that passage elevated the previous word into one of the most heroically irresistible ideas I'd ever heard or tried to comprehend in my life. I was compelled to read those Bible verses over and over and over. A self-defined heroic quest was what I'd driven myself to live my entire lifetime, so it was hard for someone like me *not* to be stopped dead in my tracks by Jesus' actual heroic words. I admit, my selfish heroic quest *had* superseded my baseline faith in Jesus. I'd literally stopped halfway to true heroism and hadn't realized it as a problem until I began to understand John 15:12-13.

On top of that, there was a massive gravity, bravado, and swagger in what Jesus was saying. His command to me was an incredibly huge concept about genuine heroic faith—something undeniably heroic in nature and intent. Jesus *was* blatantly telling me to see the heroic as He sees the heroic. And without a doubt, Jesus offered me the seemingly irrational opportunity to become like Him . . . if I obeyed Him. Beyond just my belief, if I reflected Him—after beginning to really pursue Him—Jesus *would* toss me that heroic deputy badge.

Heroic Swagger Vol. 2

Now, I knew a thing or two about real badges and the swagger that went with them. In the Box family, badges, rank, status, and authority had always been highly valued qualities.

I remember attending the Torrance California Police Academy graduation of my dad's brother, Uncle James Brent Box, when I was maybe ten or eleven years old. I remember watching as the higher ranked officers moved from one graduate to another as graduates stood at parade rest. The ranking officers would present and pin the official Torrance Police

Department badge onto each new officer, say a few brief words, shake their hand, and then move on. The graduating class maybe had between fifty to seventy-five new officers. It was a long and serious, but also a wonderful celebratory occasion.

It was amazing how that badge gave my already confident uncle even more bravado. All the same, the badge came with the responsibility to obey orders and come to attention on command. Genuinely, a police officer or deputy badge was transformative for the wearer.

The badge transferred massive privileges, but it also transferred responsibilities to the wearer. The wearer of the badge needed to reflect the truths and the values the badge represented. A police officer needed to be dedicated to upholding and obeying the laws he enforced. This was what gave an officer his swagger. For a follower of Jesus, it was the same:

A true hero *had* to reflect Jesus.

Reflect Jesus Vol. 1

"A new command I give you: Love one another. As I have loved you, so you must love one another. By this everyone will know that you are my disciples, if you love one another." —John 13:34–35, NIV

That's just it; in this analogy, the heroic deputy badge always carried with it a duty to reflect Jesus with an active faith. I hadn't properly understood this. A heroic deputy badge necessitated hustle and sweat. Yes, I was saved by my faith in Jesus, but my belief, well, my belief, absolutely required works to become heroic like Jesus is heroic.

The belief in Jesus was easy.

Genuine faith was work.

Faith without works was both dead and deadly. It had been my experience that a dead faith led me into false worship, not heroic worship.

And I had learned, false worship was poisonous to faith. It was exactly that vicious.

To be heroic as Jesus is heroic, I intended to selflessly obey in the same way Jesus obeyed God the Father, the Great Storyteller. I suppose, in this example, this is how Jesus Christ honored the heroic badge God the Father, the Great Storyteller gave Him.

It's safe to say; I could no longer *only* believe in Jesus Christ; I finally wanted to become Christlike, a disciple. And as I became more Christlike, I had no other choice. My close friendship with the Great Hero began to release His rule, power, and rest into my life. My dingy, absurd sheriff badge would be replaced by a new shiny heroic deputy badge from the Great Hero Himself. I was going to go full throttle and change the rules by which I had lived. I was going to reflect Jesus—or was I?

Reflect Jesus Vol. 2

"I'll never forget the trouble, the utter lostness, the taste of ashes, the poison I've swallowed. I remember it all—oh, how well I remember— the feeling of hitting the bottom. But there's one other thing I remember... I keep a grip on hope:"
—Lamentations 3:19-21 MSG

Sigh.

Here is a portion of a quote I shared earlier from Libbi: "Scott . . . your life is now, more than ever, about obedience. Obedience to Jesus will lead you to health." Libbi was cheering me onward to pursue and reflect Jesus into hope with unyielding, faithful determination. Health would follow. We agreed, this is what legitimate "manning up" was really all about, in the end. This would be how my new habits would be formed. Obedience to Jesus would *always* bring me new life.

I was to pursue and reflect Jesus because He expected me to. I was to love others because I was commanded to. I was to serve for the same reason. Being a proud owner of that proverbial heroic deputy badge from Jesus seemed *so* straight forward on the surface. Reflect Jesus? Easy!

"Now that I, your Lord and Teacher, have washed your feet, you also should wash one another's feet. I have set you an example that you should do as I have done for you." —John 13:14–15, NIV

So it was, I learned I had full permission to change the Frankenstein-like rules I'd created since childhood. I had learned the old sheriff's badge I felt my Dad had presented me with as a boy could be replaced by a brilliant new, truly heroic badge from Jesus Christ, Himself. But sadly, there was a *massive* problem. It was hard—no, it was impossible—to reflect Jesus as a bitter man. This might seem like it's coming out of nowhere; it did to me too: Somehow, bitterness *had* conquered me. And bitterness made its own rules.

So, you see, my bitterness didn't simply take the reflection out of the heroic deputy badge Jesus had given me; bitterness had hidden that glorious badge from me completely. So much for changing the rules, reveling in the glory of heroic deputy badges... or making progress. At least, that's how it felt in those days. Reflect Jesus? What reflection?

BITTERNESS

Bitterness Felt Like Four Letters.

I had been a Christian my entire life. I carried the label with pride. But before I could become anything like Jesus Christ and reflect Him properly—even before my story could be connected effectively to His great story—I had to get rid of the load of stinky poo-goo attached to my heart. I was carting bitterness around twenty-four hours a day, seven days a week.

Bitterness had become the rotten fruit of living through three consecutive disappointing experiences as a professional worship leader in a handful of Oregon's local churches, with a fourth short disappointment sprinkled in for good measure by the year 2014. A couple of the blows were profoundly personal and represented many of the wrongs that could occur when sociopathic narcissists became church leaders. To be fair, a couple of the disappointing experiences were just disappointing experiences, nothing more. But the bad times were awful.

The Church had triggered my bitterness. The experiences were not my fault, but bitterness *was*. I learned how bitterness felt—not only the concept of malice, but how real bitterness felt.

I had gone on a run in Redmond, Oregon, on a gorgeous but scorching summer afternoon when, seemingly out of the blue, I broke down sobbing on the side of the road. I sat down on the hot curb against a mailbox on a busy street, crying as cars drove past me. I didn't see the bitterness coming until it already had its talons deep in me. These words were going through my head on repeat:

> "So, this is what bitterness feels like . . . this is where my boiling anger, hate, and rage for how I've been treated have guided me. Jesus, please help me out of this shameful nightmare. Jesus, please help me remove my bitterness. Whoever I have to forgive, whoever I have to release, whoever I need to extend Your grace to, please help me do it!"

Over and over, I prayed something similar to that prayer as car after car splashed my puddle of tears back into my face. I was angry and confused. Still, I had to do whatever it took to release the useless bitter hate I allowed to grow in my heart toward the people that had hurt my family and me.

I didn't have the answers though. I was completely stumped because my bitterness had also made me angry with God. And while I didn't know at the moment if leaving angry with God would be an okay thing to do, I couldn't see an easy resolution coming in the next few seconds or hours as I sat on that curb. I had no shortcut to inner peace. A shortcut? No chance!

So, I got up from the curb and walked the final couple blocks home. On top of everything else, my bitterness only furthered my sense of being a heroic fraud, worship fraud, and villain all at once. I knew it. And if I knew it, then God knew it. The rules bitterness made me play by *were* rotten. Bitterness revealed the villainy in me. Bitterness felt like a four-letter word.

Darkest Days Vol. 1

If you know the biblical, Old Testament story of Jonah and the whale, I identified a bit with Jonah's frustration with God near the end of that incredible story. If you don't know the story, definitely read it for yourself (especially notice Jonah 4:6–11). Ultimately, my connection with Jonah's story wasn't the specific details, but God's overarching permission to Jonah to have real and raw feelings shared between them.

When I read the story of Jonah, I noticed, at the end of the story, Jonah was still an angry man. On top of that, I never found out if Jonah's ultimate faith in God was still intact at the end of his life. I wondered if Jonah was a hero—was he an antihero, or could he have even been a villain?

See, Jonah's story ended with him getting smacked down by God, being angry at God, and learning a lesson about how much God loved every person He'd created. I was left hanging, though. Ironically, Jonah's overall story was a redemptive story about how God, the Great Storyteller, saved an evil nation from destruction. Still, it was also a darker story about a moody and cranky man—Jonah—at the same time. So, I was curious whether Jonah ended up being redeemed *and* if he found peace with God ultimately.

In the same general way as Jonah, my story that day out on the hot curb ended in a very ambiguous way. Well, in one regard, nothing about my bitterness, anger, agitation, disappointment, and sorrow was anything close to vague—I was livid and exasperated. The shame associated with feeling like a fraud was overwhelmingly powerful, and it pulled me right into hopelessness and was driving me into spiritual death. The most cavernous sense of spiritual desperation and bitterness I'd ever encountered was the result.

So, what it came down to was I *had* to go away and come back another day for another discussion with God.

Darkest Days Vol. 2

If God did not forgive, save, and redeem, I *was* lost to Hell. If God did not allow conversations to continue over days, well, He and I wouldn't have much of a friendship then, I reasoned. If God wouldn't allow my spiritual journey to be a journey, then He was detached and merciless; I knew God wasn't detached or merciless. So that gave me some peace.

All the same, it was kind of remarkable to consider and remember all my years of work "serving" Jesus, serving the Almighty God, who I wasn't even good friends with—oh, and like Jonah, I was also very angry with God, too. Those days, the days the rules of bitterness were being challenged, were dark days.

Operation: Desperation

My realization of how bitterness had mastered me was a despairing discovery. I had never wanted to allow that seething, madness of malice I had experienced to own me. Still, somehow, bitterness *had* overpowered me. Then, when I recognized bitterness had captured me, I was overcome with disappointment for wasting even the smallest part of my life in the effort to prove I had been right and justified to hate those who had deeply wronged my family and me.

The fact was I had allowed myself to hate numerous people from my past for not loving me the way they said they loved me. They were wrong in how they treated me. But my hate was wrong, too. I had allowed myself to hate the people who hurt me for how they had made the fight so personal. In every case, I hated the injustice they seemed to be getting away with. So, I filled myself with sloppy and sticky animosity.

In a way, the realization of my bitterness was so despairing because it felt to me like I had grabbed a shovel and dug my own grave. As I was staring down into that rotten grave, I did not like what I saw—I saw a villain, Scott Wilson Box, staring blankly up at me.

Rescue Operation

But the wonder of it all is this; the recognition of my bitterness was an accelerant that caused my faith to burn faster and hotter for Jesus in the end.

After everything I had been through, the evidence of my bitterness revealed just how *desperate* I had become. I was sinful. I was mentally broken. I was working hard to get better, but I was bitter. And once I observed the ugliness of where bitterness was leading me—it was actually poisoning me spiritually, physically, and mentally—I knew I needed to be rescued by Jesus. I had to be willing to give Jesus my life in its entirety: spiritually, physically, and mentally. I needed to ask for and accept the Great Hero's rescue operation on my behalf.

My desperation and bitter villainy would bring out the best in the Great Hero. The day I chose to ask for that rescue *had* arrived.

Like a Bomb

There was a day about six months after that session on the curb when I had another intensely personal experience at a local church. I left a meeting with a lead pastor in which he had stoked the fires of bitterness in my heart with his own misguided bitterness. After a one sided exchange, I walked in stunned silence out of his office, feeling like he'd vomited on my face. After my experience that afternoon, as I was sitting in my car outside the church offices, I reached into my bag and pulled out my journal. The sun was starting to set, and it was so low in the sky it was blinding me through the windshield—a perfect metaphor for how I felt. I journaled my prayer to Jesus right there in the parking lot:

"Jesus, please begin your rescue. I need to get rid of my bitterness. This is the greatest challenge I must overcome at this stage of my life. After bitterness, Your light will reveal something else. That's okay. There will always be something else. And I welcome it. Shine Your light into my darkness right now. I see the result of bitterness in others, and I don't want that in me anywhere. Rescue me again and again and again. Because now I know, this is exactly how you rescue me and continually weave my story into Your great story of redemption. I am saved because I believe. But to this day and forever, You make the way when I obey. I get it. You rescue me and my story becomes a witness; a part of Your Story when I 'pursue Jesus, reflect Jesus.'"

A little poetic mushroom cloud blew out the top of my head. Boom.

Desperate For

My *desperation*, like layers of an onion, were becoming evident to me at last.

So yeah, I'd been at this worship leading thing as a church professional for years, doing the same churchy things for the same churchy outcomes, year in and year out, for well over a decade. Almost like the real definition of crazy, I was doing the same thing over and over, expecting a different result than I was getting. I had good intentions, but my worship was operating in the false realm of selective, ignorant, and even superstitious worship. I didn't really know Jesus as my friend because I had been so bitter—a context-killing and hope-ending combo. In a way, then, I'd been kidding myself about my impact for Jesus for years and years. What?

Does "Oh, sorry about that, God," even cover the king-sized reality of my failure?

Ultimately, bitterness had made me exhausted and defeated; I didn't know it, but bitterness was forcing me into a clumsy retreat. Yet God the Father, the Great Storyteller, *never* let me go. He was urging me to advance—*to change the rules,* to find and wield the heroic deputy badge He had tossed me with boldness.

And in an incredible twist, God used the bitterness of another man—a pastor—to help me see the hazardous danger of the bitterness in my own life. Reflexively, I made a desperate grab in my spirit for God the

Spirit, the Heroic Spirit, as if I was truly drowning. When I did, the Great Hero, Jesus Christ, rescued me.

The recognition of my bitterness had persuaded me into action, to surrender to Jesus for Him to rescue me. So, Jesus reached into my darkness and captured my attention, He guided my activity as I began to learn how to surrender my heroic Frankenstein to Him.

So, to finally understand the permission Jesus had given me to live *His* way, God the Father, the Great Storyteller, used an undeniably disarming, captivating, and unarguable true witness to help me. That witness extended from the life of a world-famous rock star . . . who was also my first cousin.

ROCKSTAR

The Rockstar

When we were kids, Brian Welch and I knew each other existed. And that was the way it remained for three decades.

In high school and early college, I didn't know my cousin was as famous as he had become. I was aware he was the lead guitarist in a serious and fairly successful rock band around the year 1996—then, by 1998, Brian Welch and the nu-metal band *Korn* had exploded onto the worldwide stage. By 1999, nominations and awards from numerous industry organizations, such as the *Grammy Awards,* skyrocketed the band's stock into the stratosphere. And it happened fast. Friends and family—heck, anyone paying attention in the music world—watched in amazement. *Korn's* music, to this day, is raw and powerful. At the turn of the millennium, their sound was unlike anything the mainstream world had ever heard. Brian was a gigantic part of creating that sound.

It's his story to tell, but it's no secret: success for Brian eventually demanded a price he could not pay. A debt of broken relationships caused by sustained substance abuse was nearly destructive. Brian dipped deep into everything the rock-star life offered, and it held him under. In many ways, his early life choices could have, perhaps should have, resulted in an early grave.

But something happened to Brian—actually, someone happened to Brian. Jesus Christ revealed himself to Brian as the only answer to the crushing life-sucking darkness inside his heart and mind. For Brian, something happened that wasn't only a feeling; it was an introduction to his Savior. He met the Great Hero, Jesus Christ. It *was* a rescue, and thankfully Brian knew he needed to be rescued.

Altered. Dumbstruck.

After Brian realized Jesus gave him permission to change the rules in his life—Brian's life was altered at a radical pace. A couple years after his journey with Jesus began, Brian wrote a very successful book titled *Save Me from Myself* that publicized his life as a child and the years he was a young man. It included his rise with *Korn*, stories about numerous personal relationships, and many of his successes and failures in provocative and occasionally shocking raw detail. I learned a lot about Brian by just reading about him, just like anyone else could.

Sure, it felt a little strange to be reading about my cousin and not just *know* my cousin . . . all the same, I did not know my cousin, so I loved reading his story about how Jesus rescued him. I was amazed by his belief, active faith, and new life.

So, after Brian began pursuing Jesus as a lifestyle, I watched as he created a new rhythm for his life. Brian was changing the rules and managing his own altered life in much the same way as my bipolar disorder and vocal cord difficulties had *forced* me to do. The main difference between Brian and me was I heard stories about him going offline to learn and study the Bible. I heard stories and saw videos friends would show me about how Brian would occasionally go ballistic to witness, share, and serve people he had never met in shopping malls, skate parks, anyplace. These were *not* things I did.

Brian was on fire, and the fire wasn't burning out, only burning hotter.

I knew Brian had defects, of course—I did too!—but I was beyond admiration for his overt dedication to become an altered man. I was dumbstruck. I was stupefied by what Jesus had done in Brian's life.

Brian was living in a way I didn't relate to. And the problem was it wasn't the rock-star aspect I couldn't figure out; it was the *following Jesus part* that was driving me a little insane.

Squinting Hard

I wondered if Brian and I both *believed* the same thing, why and how was our *faith* so different? Jesus had altered Brian so much that even a good all-American, God-fearing, professional Christian like me couldn't put my finger on exactly what I saw play out in Brian's life. I was confused.

Brian's radical actions and words were rattling not only my confidence in what I was doing as a church professional, but also just as a Christian. I was squinting hard to see something I recognized as worship, the kind of worship I understood and practiced in what Brian was doing. I didn't see much of *anything* very familiar.

But don't let my cluelessness fool you. What I saw in Brian's life were things that *were* totally valid, completely wholesome, unrestricted, and undeniably the work of Jesus—Brian's worship of Jesus was blatantly different from the worship I knew, different from the worship I was leading. His faith was definitely bigger—maybe better, I thought. I didn't know what to think.

I was perplexed by the dissimilarities and differences of the Christian worship I was leading, and that which my cousin was living. Specifically, I was trying to understand the power behind his witness for Jesus and the

Kingdom of God. I didn't have that power. I wondered, "How is Brian's faith and witness connected to worship?"

Witness

Yes, I knew Jesus had permitted Brian to change the rules he had lived in his life. But, I knew innately, for Brian, his faith in Jesus Christ, the Great Hero, couldn't have been about being a slave to a bunch of whacky new rules or having years of Bible education—it *had* to have been about self-discipline, obedient sacrifice, and his personal desire to pursue Jesus. Brian was either putting on a stupid show for attention, or this was a genuine quest. If he was being genuine, then Brian's quest had to be about his desperation to be saved by Jesus Christ. This is what I reasoned, and go figure, Brian's lifestyle proved his quest for Jesus was the truth. Brian *was* being changed.

And the change I saw in Brian made it clear that desperation for Jesus—to pursue Jesus into a friendship—was all that was necessary to qualify anyone to reflect Jesus, to be a witness.

Something clicked into place.

If you've ever had a dislocated joint, it was like experiencing the enormous relief once the joint was relocated—click, click. Brian's lifestyle of heroic worship—pursuing and reflecting Jesus as a friend—put on display something I'd been seeking for, you know, almost every day I could remember:

The reflection of Jesus was the only way to achieve true heroism.

And *there was no way to be truly heroic without first being a true worshiper, a person who pursues Jesus.*

Now, I'm almost positive heroism didn't matter to Brian. He wasn't thinking about his pursuit of Jesus through the same heroic lens I was. All the same, Brian's new life and lifestyle indicated to me that the faithful pursuit of Jesus was the first and only necessary qualification for the reflection of Jesus. Because of Brian's pursuit and reflection of Jesus, I began to understand true worship seemed to be divinely linked to true heroism in this exact fashion.

The rock star's redeemed lifestyle proved to me true worship, pursuing Jesus, and true heroism, reflecting Jesus, was the *only way* to be a simple, effective, and sustainable Christian witness.

It was Brian who provided me with the most concrete example of what it would look like for me to surrender my life to Jesus. To be an effective witness like Brian, I needed a heroic form of worship.

> *"But you will receive power when the Holy Spirit comes upon you. And you will be my witnesses, telling people about me everywhere—in Jerusalem, throughout Judea, in Samaria, and to the ends of the earth." —Acts 1:8, NLT*

Brian demonstrated to me that it **takes everything** to be an Acts 1:8 witness to the world . . . because it's supposed to.

Bullseye

Most Christians would agree they believe Acts 1:8 identifies a Christian's heroic duty to be a witness. I agree. Sadly, I was one of the many people who were mostly wrong about the verse's application for years of my life. Even though I had been looking right at it, I'd been blinded by my heroic Frankenstein and selfishness. I had been mostly wrong because I didn't understand the humble *desperation* I had to have for Jesus, to be an Acts 1:8 witness to the world. Plain and simple, *I wasn't pursuing Jesus in a way I could reflect Jesus.* I hadn't surrendered myself to Jesus, really. I was looking right past the Great Hero, Jesus Christ. My church worship had to do with music—planning, preparing, playing, and singing songs; leading teams of song leaders; planning service orders; saying prayers; conducting weekly rituals; pleasing lead pastors; more and more hunting for new songs; and singing even more songs. "Worship" meant pretty much anything I wanted it to mean, almost everything *other than* an outright lifestyle of pursuing a friendship with Jesus.

My form of Christian worship included all sorts of good and even useful things, but my forms of worship were *incomplete*. Heck, my worship may often have even been false worship . . .

It wasn't more singing or leading people in songs that would make me a true worshiper. Surely, it wasn't the writing and recording of one more heartfelt ballad or praise song, either! Like David hit Goliath between the eyes with the stone, I understood the bullseye of true worship: *only* pursuing Jesus could make me a true worshiper; a true witness.

I was finally nearing the eternal heroic bullseye I'd been hunting for my whole life. True heroism required I surrender and sacrifice *everything* to Jesus to worship properly. I *had* to pursue friendship with Jesus with a balls-to-the-wall lifestyle. Nothing else I called "worship" would be true worship.

I had learned a great humiliation as a Christian leader:

I believed in Jesus. I knew about Jesus. But I wasn't friends with Jesus! As a Christian worship professional and as a supposed follower of Jesus, if things remained the same, I would never experience the joy of becoming a witness like my cousin had become. Wicked bitterness could not disable my witness any longer than it already had.

Put as plainly as I can; to become a heroic worshiper like Jesus, I *had to* "Pursue Jesus." to "Reflect Jesus."

Bullseye.

Rock-Star Worship Leader

I was late for the game, but eventually, I became astonished by Jesus Christ, the Great Hero. By watching my rock-star cousin's imperfect and yet heroic quest to pursue and reflect Jesus, I had seen something I could not unsee—I had learned something I never wanted to unlearn. I finally had traction where I hadn't had any grip for years.

In my story, even if I didn't entirely know what the truth about true worship and true heroism would demand of me down the road, I was permanently willing to risk a goofy-footed pursuit of Jesus. I was ready to risk looking like a moronic fool in the reflection of Jesus. I desperately desired my heroism and my worship to be true. I wanted my witness to be a reflection of the Great Hero, Jesus Christ, *not* my heroic Frankenstein!

To sum this all up, I wanted to begin to see worship as Jesus sees worship. I wanted to see heroic as Jesus sees heroic, and I was desperate to be heroic as Jesus is heroic. I was desperate for Jesus to be my friend like I had never been desperate for His friendship before. I was desperate to bury my villainy of bitterness forever. The difference between Brian's witness and my witness was that he was truly desperate for Jesus to save him. I hadn't been.

Further, I didn't yet know Jesus Christ, the Great Hero, really. But I wanted to. And if my rock-star cousin could, I would. Additionally, Jesus Christ, the Great Hero, compelled me—like He compelled my cousin, Brian "Head" Welch—to tell my story. To become a witness.

"I found something worth dying for. I was so foolishly in love. I was gonna tell everybody." —Brian "Head" Welch

I finally knew there was nothing for me to be angry or bitter about. There was only Jesus to be desperate for. I was being drawn closer and closer to Jesus as I pursued Him. The attraction became stronger and stronger.

The rock star had led the worship leader.

TRAUMA

Grisly. Gruesome.

On Friday, June 6, 2014, I heard a traumatic and painful story from my dad. He called me from his office at Seattle Pacific University (SPU). Dad always took my calls, but he rarely called me during the workday. I answered his call anxiously.

The day before, on Thursday afternoon, a gunman forced his way into the foyer of an educational building on the campus of SPU and shot three students, killing one. The gunman was tackled to the ground by a twenty-two-year-old building monitor. If I had space, I'd write a whole chapter about this heroic young man who risked his life to save the lives of numerous other students.

As a career-long SPU administrator, Dad was horror-struck—he knew he could do nothing about the grisly and gruesome outcome of the shooting, and his compassion for the students and community around the SPU organization was overflowing. Dad also felt enormous empathy for the emotional trauma the young man who faced down the shooter to protect others would endure. He felt overcome with grief for the wounded and the family and friends of the young man who was killed.

Dad struggled with the thought of any student trapped in those terrifying moments. Dad was heartbroken for his administrative friends and coworkers who would be in the direct line of a different kind of unsettling fire: handling the emergency personnel, the communication with the community, families, and the media. Most of all, Dad could only imagine the immeasurable weight and crushing humility those moments and the months ahead would demand from one or two of his closest administrative colleagues. The realization of the impossibility of offering any service or love that could eliminate the loss, the fear, the pain, or the anger of the parents, families, loved ones, and the entire SPU institution was immediate. There would be *no* easy heroic answers—even the understanding and practice of worship was confused and tense. For the indefinite future, there would be an overwhelming cluster of chaos.

Overwhelmed

Now, Dad had trusted Jesus with a great, lasting, and ever-maturing faith from childhood. Dad had also trusted the mysterious balance between God's loving, all-knowing great plans and purpose intersecting with the repercussions and evils of mankind's free will. Dad understood it all intellectually. He believed it spiritually. And Dad had seen and lived through plenty of awful things, but this event at SPU was deeply personal. In some ways, it bypassed intellect and was a furious direct assault on his heart, on his spirit. In the history of Seattle Pacific University, there might have been people who loved the institution as much as Dad, but *no one* loved the university or was prouder of it than him. Dad bled maroon—hex color #892F49—and white. Yes, he did.

Dad had given much of his life to honor, proudly represent, and protect his SPU family. Because of the nature of his job in University Advancement (fundraising), Dad probably knew three, maybe four, successive generations of SPU alumni all at once—many of them personally. That was the key. Dad was relationally invested in the lives of an entire organization, a whole family. For Dad, an attack on SPU was only the slightest bit different from an attack on Mom, Mandy, Brad, or me.

Now, people didn't pick fights with our family because Tom Box was an intimidating enemy; he was big and strong, yet also smart and strategic. Plus, Dad had powerful friends, too. Picking a fight with Dad would not have been much different from trying to poke holes in General Patton's Third United States Army during World War II.

A deadly assault such as what happened at SPU would have caused every "heroic" nerve within Dad to be activated. It would've privately tortured him to not first protect or respond with swift eye-for-an-eye fury—not because it was his responsibility, but because his reflexive all-American, God-fearing "heroic" character had been triggered. The event cut to the quick, cut to his heart. Dad was in deep emotional pain. His university family had been attacked and injured. A SPU family member had been killed. The shooting tested Dad's witness.

There's no other way to explain it, there were many emotions on the field of battle that day Dad and I talked, not the least of which was shame. Rightly or wrongly, an all-American, God-fearing hero like Dad would have felt something very close to humiliation when he realized he was not capable of responding as the hero he expected himself to be. It didn't matter if the realization had occurred in either a neutral and safe moment or a truly dark one beset by evil; any moment of heroic inadequacy would be knee-buckling because of its presumed indignity and loss of pride.

But *instead*, in my conversation with Dad, I experienced the most intense humility and desperation I had ever heard from him before that day.

Near the end of our talk, Dad took a long breath and almost whispered; "Scotter, would you do me a favor and listen to the song 'Overwhelmed,' by the band Big Daddy Weave?" Surprised, I asked in response, "Right now?"

"Yes, please," Dad responded. "I don't want to bother you, but will you pull it up on YouTube real quick? I just want to listen to it together."

So, with no other talk, we started the song separately on either end of the phone. When Dad heard the music start on my end, he started the song on his computer. My run of the song was a couple of seconds ahead of Dad's. It was a bit distracting, but I knew it was important. I continued to listen to the song with a heavy heart.

After years of watching each other navigate our heroic quests, navigating all the trips and traps of hero duty as best as we could, Dad didn't need to tell me anything about what he felt—we just felt it together, without speaking. In those moments, before our phone call had ended, Dad and I were covered by a heroic blanket of musical praise to Jesus.

As the song was nearing its end, Dad had been silent. He then quietly sniffed, "I love you, my son. I'm so proud of you. Thank you for this time together. I've got to go."

I may have seen Dad cry two or three times in my entire life. I couldn't see him over the phone, but I could tell he was tearing up on his end. I knew it was time for the call to end, too.

I always called Dad "Daddy" as a child, and it followed me into adulthood; "I love you, Daddy," rolled quickly off my tongue as we ended the call.

Bigger Picture

"Show me a hero, and I'll write you a tragedy."
—F. Scott Fitzgerald, 1945, Notebook E.

For my dad, this hideous event could have caused him to power up. Dad could have been guided by pride and anger. That would have been a spiritual tragedy. His witness would have been tarnished.

For Dad, leaving his all-American, God-fearing heroism behind might have even felt a bit disgraceful. But this would be no tragedy—it was magical. The great story of redemption had magically intersected with Dad's heroic quest.

The truly heroic things of Jesus shaped my dad. Jesus overwhelmed him. *Pride would call Dad's quest a tragedy, but humility made his desperation shameless.* And that's pretty much miraculous for a man like Tom Box.

Context Vol. 1

I want to put this all into context. Dad and I both pursued heroism as purpose, as duty. Striving to become virtuous, heroic warriors dedicated to our hero duty was a noble pursuit on the surface. We thought *that* would be our witness for Jesus. We were wrong.

Dad and I eventually realized the All-American, God-fearing, heroic standard we were aiming for was a moving target. And yet, the pursuit hadn't been entirely fruitless. As I mentioned at the beginning of this story, the context and definitions we had operated with got us halfway there, halfway to true heroism. And I imagine that's why it felt like we achieved progress for so many years.

For Dad, it had taken an overwhelming crisis to make his final adjustment and embrace the correct context of God the Father, the Great Storyteller.

In my case, my failure to understand my correct context was what led to my life's most supreme moments of horrifying shame, disappointment, and angst. Those were the days fear and shame gripped me with a wicked, caustic embrace. I eventually realized the correct context would have made all the difference all those years earlier.

Context Vol. 2

When I reference my correct context, here's what I mean. If God's everlasting existence had been my context for the heroism I pursued for the first decades of my life, miserable, *selfish ambition* would not have deceived me and created a heroic Frankenstein. I would have realized the Great Storyteller, the "everlasting to everlasting"—as the Israelite leader Moses describes God in Psalm 90—meant something very personal and eternal when He created me. Eventually, I did understand that Jesus' context began to release the magic of heroic worship into my life . . . and that was mind-blowing.

The Magic

For years and years, I was trying to write myself in as an all-American, God-fearing hero, as a winner and not a villain—I wanted "heroic winner" to be my story. The thing is, I was trying to create my own purpose, only I was a hamster on a spinning wheel of sickening stress. I was trying to make my own meaning, and this mattered as I aged because my "heroic" striving began to develop a ravine between the context of my heroic Frankenstein and God's indescribable, everlasting to everlasting context. There is so much to try to unpack about this topic; what remains of this story would suffer if I tried to expand. So for now, it's best to only simply share what absolutely mystified me:

The monstrous wreckage of my heroic Frankenstein would forever have led me to be too broken to be a hero, too sinful to be a worshiper, and too fearful to be hopeful. This is the *real* reason I needed to be rescued by the Great Hero, Jesus Christ—I hadn't known my correct context so it had been *impossible* to know my purpose, or even how to be a witness. Shame and painful on-the-ground realities had finally forced a desperation in my life that drove me to want to be rescued by Jesus. The fog of war was clearing.

Drilling one final level deeper into the magic of it all:

When I looked closely I saw the heroism and worship of Jesus showed me the nature, character, and values of God.

Fundamentally, Jesus showed me exactly *who* God is. And because Jesus *was* a heroic worshiper, there was no way around the fact, heroic worship *was* from everlasting to everlasting. Correct context *was* everything! What this all came down to, and what I was astounded to realize I had learned was, the deep magic of heroic worship *preexisted* mankind, even all creation. Heroic worship *was* the very nature and character of the everlasting to everlasting, God the Father, the Great Storyteller, God the Son, and God the Spirit. Heroic worship is what God valued most from His creation and somehow, what He also valued within the very members of the everlasting to everlasting Trinity, Himself. Jesus revealed something awe-inspiring, hopeful, and inconceivably magical:

Heroic worship was good-guy magic, the greatest and deepest of all magic.

And I was divinely designed to live my story as a heroic worshiper like Jesus Christ, the Great Hero, lived His story as a heroic worshiper.

Great Storyteller

"Because that's what we storytellers do. We restore order with imagination. We instill hope again and again and again."
—Walt Disney; Saving Mr. Banks, directed by
John Lee Hancock, 2013

After having dinner and cleaning up, Mom and Dad would call Mandy, Brad, and me into the family room, typically closer to bedtime. We would gather at the end of the day to say prayers and listen to Dad read a chapter or two from famous twentieth-century scholar and author C. S. Lewis' fantasy books, *The Chronicles of Narnia*. Over time, we kids and Mom eventually heard all seven of the Narnia stories read to us in Dad's smooth, natural delivery. The more popular of the seven books were *The Lion, the Witch and the Wardrobe*, along with *Prince Caspian* and *The Voyage of The Dawn Treader*. Maybe you've read these stories or seen the movies they inspired? Perhaps you even had them narrated to you as we did.

I loved listening to Dad transport us into a secret, fantastic land with heroic talking beasts, lampposts in the forest, and dark powers that threatened noble, honest, and just creatures. Listening to Dad read those stories helped me become sensitive to the truth of God's greatness, and they eventually aided me in pinpointing the correct context for life in sinful chaos.

See, my parents didn't raise me with the fear of magical things. Maybe it was because magic was synonymous with the war between good versus evil; all-American, God-fearing heroism understood this reality, but Jesus' heroism was immeasurably equipped for good versus evil. Jesus understood the treacherous clutches of generational evil like no other could.

Good-guy magic represented God's everlasting-to-everlasting power. In Narnia, the power of Aslan, the giant golden lion—the Jesus Christ character—could *never* be overcome. This was the most excellent news, as it meant all other magic—bad-guy magic—was far less potent than good-guy magic; In other words, though deadly, bad-guy magic could only mimic and pretend to be more powerful than the most fearful of all magic, good-guy magic. The proper healthy context for magic played a giant role in the stories of my childhood.

The magic of the Great Storyteller, God the Father, had no expiration date. Bad-guy magic had an end date.

The Good Guys Win

In the world and tales of Narnia, good and evil were in conflict for control and in a perpetual tug-of-war. I never knew how it would play out as

Dad read those stories, yet I always believed that, when all was said and done, good would triumph over evil. Eventually, as each book ended, I was right—good would win. But for good to win, there was *always* a cost. I didn't fully understand the connection in those days, but I started to put it together quickly the more we read the stories.

Aspects of free will and the allure of bad-guy magic led to loss, pain, and many bad things; the truth was almost always obscured by dark lies and evil characters or horrifying events.

Even as a child, I learned life would have many chapters and seasons, just like those Narnia books did. I welcomed them—chapters and seasons gave me hope. And I knew that even though evil might seem to often overcome good, it ultimately could not. Good won. The Great Hero, Jesus Christ, *had* won. He had overcome and brought order to the chaos. Jesus' victory brought all things into the correct context; the everlasting to everlasting Great Storyteller wrote the beginning, middle, and the end of His great story of redemption. The mystery was that He allowed heroic worshipers to write themselves *into* the great, everlasting story, while villains would write themselves into eternal chaos.

Frankenstein loses. The good guys win.

Heroic Disgrace Vol. 1

Jesus expected me to be a hero. Only, Jesus expected me to be heroic *His* way. And Jesus' way was the way—seemingly—of total disgrace. After all, the Great Hero's disgrace *was* the cross. But the cross was *also* His heroism! Huh? It was all so full of contradiction and irony on the surface.

For years and years, I had believed in Jesus, but I often saw His form of heroism as being degrading and even embarrassing. Like so many others throughout history, the cross looked to me to be the most shamefully humiliating thing that could have happened to Jesus. "Why did He have to be heroic *that* way?" I questioned. William Barclay offered me a power-ful perspective:

> "The cross was the final battle of Jesus with the powers of evil.
> But He was not afraid of it, for He knew that evil had no ultimate
> power over Him. He went to His death in the certainty, not of
> defeat, but of conquest."
> —Barclay's Daily Study Bible, John 14:25–31

So the cross *was* a heroic necessity. And the cross fit Jesus Christ, the Great Hero's, definition of heroism perfectly:

> *"This is my commandment: Love each other in the same way I have
> loved you. There is no greater love than to lay down one's life for
> one's friends." —John 15:12–13, NLT*

The cross was the unimaginably upside-down representation of Jesus' heroism and worship. And the Great Hero's sacrifice for me on that cross was the eternal remedy for my mental brokenness, unhealthy habits, all the chaos around me, all the fear within me, and all the disgusting sin-fulness clinging to me. The actions of Jesus seemed disgraceful—maybe. But His love was heroic—absolutely.

That was the glorious nature of heroic disgrace in a nutshell. So like Jesus, Heroic disgrace needed to become *my* witness too.

Heroic Disgrace Vol. 2

To be heroic as Jesus is heroic, I had to willingly—obediently—offer the Great Hero, Jesus Christ, all my real-life disgrace. I needed to stop playing whack-a-mole with my selfishness, bitterness, and disobedience. It was the only thing that made any sense for me to me to do. To be heroic as Jesus is heroic, I had to obey Him, no matter the disgrace something like my various types of prideful kryptonite—parent pleasing or heroic fraud—might cause me to feel. Jesus' heroic disgrace—the cross and His resurrection—*had* saved me, so the least I could do was embrace the upside-down paradox of heroic disgrace.

Don't get lost in the weeds here.

To be heroic like Jesus is heroic, I *had* to embrace heroic disgrace *the way* Jesus did, as best as I could. I had to!

When I embraced heroic disgrace, I finally began to live my life with the correct context—I became properly desperate for Jesus to save the day, every day. I gave up trying to be the kind of hero that saved the day myself. I had to give everything, all of it. And *this* was my purpose. Please don't miss my point here.

My desperate surrender to Jesus—slavery to *my* Great Hero—made *me* heroic royalty.

Heroic worship is pure magic, the deepest kind.

The Upside Down

Everything I had known felt so inverted, yet it still seemed so right at the same time—that is, I could only write myself into the great story of redemption through things that seemed completely upside down, through seemingly disgraceful things: through humility, not pride; through submission, not strength; through slavery, not mastery; through being the least, not the greatest; through being the last in line, not the first; through selflessness, not selfishness; and through giving myself away, not demanding my way. Demanding my way made me a bad guy, and bad guys don't win in the end. At the end of the great story of redemption, bad guys became the truly disgraced.

I knew my brokenness had disgraced me. In far too many ways, I had lived a lifetime as a disgraced bad guy.

But because I pursued and reflected Jesus as His friend, Jesus flipped my disgrace upside down—He was the good guy. It was Jesus' "disgrace," the heroism of the cross, that had rescued me. *Correct context **was** everything.*

Three streams in my life had intersected and created a tsunami of understanding: Bipolar disorder, my heroic Frankenstein, and incomplete or false worship. To be clear, the brokenness I experienced with my bipolar disorder had opened my eyes to my twisted view of both heroism and worship. I was laid bare. Then Jesus, the Great Hero, remade me. I found new life. Ironically, I went from disgrace to disgrace to find His grace, mercy, peace, and hope in my new life. There is no way to describe my joy for having been so broken, so upside down.

Heroic Like Jesus

Though it didn't start that way, my attraction to Jesus became an obsession. For years, I allowed my mental descent into acute bipolar II disorder and bitterness to pull me away and make me insecure and . . . feel insane. But the day had come when obediently choosing to be heroic like Jesus is heroic became the *only* sane thing for me to do. I was finally getting it. There was something magical about my focus on *aligning my habits* toward new life and endless adventure . . . it *was* taking everything to be heroic like Jesus.

To confirm the great lessons I had learned, here's a quick review:

To be heroic as Jesus is heroic, it came down to; I needed to worship as the Great Hero worshiped. And because Jesus modeled heroic worship between Him and God the Father, it was clear what the definition of heroic worship was: "Pursue Jesus. Reflect Jesus." as a habit leading to hope. Jesus modeled this exact process in his life; *Jesus pursued the Father. Jesus reflected the Father; in everything.* And Jesus never lost hope, even when the heroic path He was on seemed to be paved with disgrace. Instead, Jesus was focused on new life and endless adventure for His creation. His reward for

His faithful obedience was to return to eternity and sit at the right hand of God the Father. Wondrous.

I knew from observation and experience; heroic worship was the road less traveled. Heroic worship made a person a witness like my cousin had been for me. And my experience also proved to me; heroic worship was the course of personal—mind, body, and spirit—health, the hope of sacrificial unity, revival in the Church, everlasting hope, and eternal reward. Heroic worship "takes everything" because it connects *all* things—the deepest of all magic.

Because I was determined to be heroic like Jesus, heroic worship also led me to the most astonishing and seemingly impossible possibility; the heroic magnetism of the Cross of Jesus Christ. The disgrace of the Cross and the heroism of the Resurrection gave my story, doubtless eternal hope.

Thankfully, my obsession with heroic worship caused the magnetic poles to flip from fear and despair to unending hope. It was a good thing, too; I was going to need another stiff dose of hopeful certainty.

DEATH

We Shook on It

Since I was maybe seven or eight years old, Dad and I created and shared a special handshake. Years later, after countless handshakes, Dad experienced a close call when he had a pulmonary embolism and spent a couple of nights in the hospital. He and I had a short, sweet, but cherished talk one of those evenings. As we talked, Dad struggled with the mental weight of being a mortal man—maybe even more than others—I think. But like most anyone, Dad's pulmonary embolism made him fully aware any future goodbye might be our last goodbye. We admitted that there might never be an opportunity for a clearly defined final greeting . . . or farewell handshake.

So, that night in the hospital, with very few words, Dad and I agreed we would say our final goodbye with our eyes every single time we were together from then on. And then we shook on it.

Then we both did it. Every visit, we did it—every single one.

For ten years, it was always the same. It was subtle. It was necessary. And it was beautiful to share that kind of simple, lasting, eternal intimacy with Dad.

We'd catch each other's eyes, linger half a moment longer than usual before getting in the car, shutting the front door, or disconnecting from a video call. We'd purse our lips, partially grin, swallow hard, nod slightly, then get back to bringing order to the chaos in the world around us both.

Damn you, death. I loved that man.

Yes, Jesus

All of mankind's stories have a last page. All journeys end. All heroes die. But all truly heroic stories are eternal.

On the morning of October 9, 2018, my brother Brad called from Salem, Oregon, to share the news that our dad experienced a massive stroke while doing a puzzle that morning with my brother's children. Not long after Dad collapsed, the Great Hero took Thomas Wilson Box into eternity. I assure you, it was a heroic, even gallant, homecoming.

Before he breathed his last, my dad looked my brother in the eye as they prayed together. When Brad finished his prayer, Dad, loosely holding to his youngest son, murmured, "Ysss, Jsss." In a testament to his trust in Jesus, even at the very end, with all his remaining might, Dad took a ferocious swing of his heroic sword as a reflection of Jesus—a selfless obedient servant—one final time. This time, he gave death the foot, the only way he was still able . . . "Ysss, Jssss." A glorious "Yes, Jesus."

"Jesus called out with a loud voice, 'Father, into your hands I commit my spirit.' When He had said this, He breathed His last." —Luke 23:44–46

Titanic

"True love, Tinker Bell's pixie dust,

From nursery to star to Neverland.

True love, a hero's departure

To eternal waves and golden sands.

Oh, Greatest Hero! Come again!

Oh, Greatest Hero! Come again!" —S. W. Box

Speaking of golden sands, ocean beaches, glorious light . . . and icebergs.

While in Dad's hospital room the night of his stroke, the family and I were patiently awaiting his body's slow shutdown after being taken off the ventilator. It wasn't fun—heck, it was like the sinking of the Titanic. His body was snoring and relaxed like he was sleeping back at home. It reminded me of the crazy reality of the violence under the waterline of the Titanic. I remembered the stories about how the engineers and ser-vicemen worked as if they were going to stop the inevitable. They couldn't. Because the damage was so significant, those men could do nothing to save the ship. They worked until the sea consumed them, and even the band valiantly played right up until the very last moment. Their last song was "Nearer My God to Thee." I felt the all-star "Boy Scout," the Hoss—my dad—was like the sinking Titanic.

As the night continued, I decided to shove in a few soft earplugs and lay down to try to sleep in the corner of the room. As I closed my eyes, I couldn't get the image of the Titanic out of my mind. I hated it. I prayed to God that He would help me think of something much more buoyant.

Then in a flash, that brutal imagery became something brighter and more colorful. It was just like Peter Pan said, "Oh, and something I forgot. Dust! Yep, just a little bit of pixie dust. Now think of the happiest things. It's the same as having wings." It's a bit goofy to admit even now, but it's true; I got a vision of Dad having already arrived in Eternity. It was refreshing. It was exciting. It was magical. And it was hopeful.

Oceans

In this vision, the Titanic wasn't sinking—it had already sunk. The Titanic was in the deep dark and resting at the bottom of the ocean. What was done was done.

It may not have seemed like it, but this image of a sunken Titanic allowed me to realize the moment I had been fearing had already passed. Dad had kicked in the door. He had already crossed the veil between death and into new eternal and heroic life. The golden sand of the eternal shores was already on Dad's feet. Dad's earthly body, slowly shutting down, was just following the lead of his soul. And his soul had left the building.

Right then and there, in that dark room, I pictured Dad making the transition from Earth to Heaven. The imagery I had was of him arriving on the shores of eternity much the same way a giddy kid arrives at the beach on a late summer morning, throwing everything from the car in a sandy pile for his parents to organize and arrange on the beach. I pictured Dad kicking up sand behind him as he darted for the waves and waters of his new home, then I smiled as if I heard Jesus shouting out a needless reassurance to my dad from the parking lot; "Hey! I got your family back on the other side. Celebrate with everyone waiting to say 'Hi' to you on this side." I imagined Dad peering out into the water with tremendous anticipation—he was soaking up the glory of the place and starting to glow. In my mind's eye, I saw Dad glowing.

Laying there in that corner, I was having a full-blown daydream at this point. I dreamed Dad never let up from his sprint across the sand. Then, as he splashed up to his knees in the water, he dove into the spray and foam of the heavenly ocean, throwing himself under the first wave and popping up with complete abandon and joy on the other side. I pictured his brother and his dad joining him. I envisioned each of my great-grandparents swimming alongside Dad too. I saw friends who had passed through the eternal heavenly veil before Dad circling and splashing around in the water next to him.

No, Dad wasn't sinking like the Titanic—that was old news. Instead, it was as if I could see Dad rising with and riding the bright ocean surf in triumph. Dad was not only at peace, but he was also filled with joy. He was seeing the outcome of his friendship with Jesus, of his heroic worship. Dad was only beginning to grasp the unfathomable extent of his endless options to reflect Jesus in true heroism as a selfless and obedient servant for all of eternity. I could see it vividly as I dreamed; I felt the joy of being a heroic worshiper in eternity, the surge of unending mystery and adventure. Most of all, I heard the glad vibrations of the fearless, eternal echo rumbling from Aslan's Country into the Shadowlands of this world.

God the Father, the Great Storyteller, spoke into my imagination and brought order to the agonizing chaos that surrounded me the night Dad died—so, pardon me, but this seemed at the moment to have been a titanic vision. Hope *was* titanic.

He's Gone

This vision gave me chills. It brought me to tears. I dreamed Dad had made it, that he had made it to the oceans of eternity. It had been a spectacular vision of joy and crazy celebration when I genuinely needed it. All of Heaven was giving a hero's welcome to a new saint, a heroic worshiper.

So, I wiped the tears from my face and, with a grin and a sigh, rolled to my other side. I napped a bit longer in the soft glow of the nighttime lighting of the hospital room, grieving but strangely at peace.

At one point later that night, in my restless attempt at getting a little sleep, I sensed a stirring in the hospital room that made me open my eyes. The room was still dim, but I pulled my earplugs from my ears and got up from my mid-night nap. The nurse was whispering and looking my mom in the eye as I walked to the side of Dad's bed. I arrived just as Dad's body took its final shallow breath. Moments later, his heart beat its last beat. The nurse turned off the heart monitor and was quietly, calmly, and gently talking the family through the moment; "Here it is, friends. It's time. He's gone." Only a few minutes back, it might have seemed to me like the Titanic had only just crossed under the waves. It could have been crushing.

But in my mind and my heart, I had seen a heroic worshiper's first moments in his new heroic home—a heroic blessing from God the Father, the Great Storyteller.

Blowing Away the Kryptonite Vol. 1

It's always a bit staggering to be reminded that life goes on. Heroes die. Violent winds still blow storms. Warm summer breezes come and go. And everyone living still breathes in, out, in, out . . .

I stood at the head of Dad's hospital bed after the nurse moved all the bedside equipment into the far corner of the room. His body was still and genuinely at peace, so I slipped my hand behind Dad's freshly barbered head of hair. I could still feel the warmth of his body's death struggle. Though invisible to me, the massive stroke that had turned Dad's heroic lights out was only millimeters from my palm. I bent down and kissed his sweaty forehead. "I love you, Daddy. Thank you, sir—thank you for everything," I needlessly whispered in his ear. I stopped myself from crying by swallowing hard. I furrowed my forehead, closed my eyes, and some kind of choked snort came from behind my nose. I breathed deep and let it out slowly. I watched my breath blow across Dad's red hair, parted and combed just as he had brushed it that morning before sitting down to do that puzzle with his grandchildren for the last time.

Interestingly, like a bad memory and a regression into a bad habit, a familiar and unwelcome responsibility blew into my mind at that moment.

It was as if a chunk of kryptonite had blown in with a strong wind. The kryptonite landed somewhere near me—a reflex: I had to replace Dad! I had to fill his shoes. I had to keep it all together. I had to come through, or else. I had to please Dad, or else . . .

Blowing Away the Kryptonite Vol. 2

It was like I hit an iceberg. Frigid water was pouring into the hull of my mind, and the freezing wind made me hold my breath. I felt instant fear.

Wait . . . or else *what*? I thought to myself. I was *literally* standing over Dad's dead body. I hit the emotional emergency brake and immediately plugged the damage from the figurative iceberg that had punctured the hull of my brain. I caught myself from going any further down that emotionally debilitating kryptonite-filled black hole in real time. I stopped myself going down like the sinking ship I had only recently pictured in my head. I stopped the heroic Frankenstein from being reanimated. Instead, I kicked the heroic monster and kryptonite overboard and let them sink into the depths—sinful, fear-filled pride was *not* going to defeat me in that moment. Instead, I let the peaceful tropical wind blowing off the oceans of Aslan's Country guide my thoughts, not fear. Not anger. Not selfishness or bad habits.

I had already lived and released the burden of needing to become something or someone I couldn't have been years ago. With years of support from my wife and lots of professional help from Arvilla and Libbi, I had removed myself from the kryptonite of a self-imposed belief I needed to be a Hoss to please my dad and avoid any disapproval from him or others in my family. It had always been a brutal fight at the moment, but this time, I was free of the burden as if it had never been a struggle in the first place.

I threw myself humbly into Jesus with desperation, the way I had learned was necessary so many numerous times over the years. Instead of a pathetic fight with my many weaknesses or villainy, the tricky moment came and went. In a way, I felt like the man—the fearless man—I wanted to be, the one I'd pursued from childhood to Kariann's and my wedding to well into those early days of our marriage, but I hadn't achieved.

At that moment, the love of Jesus had cast out fear in an instant. Warm winds calmed my grief and any panic. Desperation for Jesus gave me peace and rest I could not have anticipated. So, there I was, my first layer of kryptonite—parent pleasing—shattered and sunk. It ended right then and there that very night. My second layer of kryptonite, heroic fraud, had also shattered and sunk, its cruel grip ended right then and there that very night, too.

Instead, I stood next to Dad's peaceful body knowing for a fact he had lived proud of me. He died proud of me. He lived his final years knowing he and I had traveled a truly heroic adventure together as different people, yet equally dependent upon Jesus Christ, the Great Hero. And at that moment, I had caught myself from allowing those aspects of my prideful kryptonite access into my life anymore. I caught myself from testing the borders of bitterness.

Wow, I caught myself! And I didn't need Dad's quick reflexes or any of our all-star trophies. It was a decisive moment. It was another surreal moment in a day full of astounding moments. It was the Great Hero's gift to me in those emotionally complicated minutes, and I accepted the gift.

END OF THE STORY

Passing the Test

Dad's death gave heroic worship its first real test; Dad's death forced me to take something seemingly abstract and apply it to a very harsh reality. Heroic worship had to either move out of the conceptual realm to the realm of all things definite and very material, *or* it would move into the trash.

And while I found death didn't erase all the good—or even lasting—things Tom Box did, death made all those things feel basically meaningless in his absence. I didn't care about Dad's accomplishments or legacy. I didn't care about his invisible HERO badge, trophies, or the bootstraps he tugged to charge ahead in his all-American, God-fearing heroism for so many years—I just wanted Dad. I cared about Dad's love for me. I cared about not being able to call Dad when I was in pain. I cared that my childhood hero was dead. I cared for my children—all my family—would have a giant hole in their lives, as I did, and would have to go on living without him.

So heroic worship had a nearly impossible task to achieve, I thought.

But pursuing and reflecting Jesus as a habit leading to hope was *far* more powerful than I gave it credit for initially; heroic worship formed a lens through which I saw God the Father, God the Son, and God the Spirit in an entirely new way. Heroic worship caused me to see God for who He really was—in His brilliant everlasting-to-everlasting correct context. That divine moment of eternal genesis created in my heart by the scripture John 3:16, from the Holy Bible, had never been extinguished; *". . . that whoever believes in Him [Jesus] shall not perish, but have eternal life."* Jesus offers new life and endless adventure to those who pursue and reflect Him.

Wielding the Sword

I had a dad who believed in Jesus and took the lead to pursue and reflect Him as a habit leading to hope in his eternal destiny; a hope in Heaven, a yearning for Aslan's Country—an eternity in Heaven—a yearning for the adventurous sunrise of new life.

Dad didn't have it all perfected or figured out on the day he died. He pursued and reflected Jesus until the end, not perfectly, but consistently. Yes, he had to overcome many wrong ideas and useless all-American, God-fearing, presumptions about heroism, but Dad always trusted Jesus. Dad was faithful and obedient to pursue and reflect Jesus as a habit leading to hope—this was the sword he practiced with and then wielded in battle. For everything else, Dad worked past his pride to humbly believe and allow Jesus to become his defender in an overwhelming way.

> *"The LORD your God, who is going before you, will fight for*
> *you . . . before your very eyes . . ." —Deuteronomy 1:30, NIV*

I was proud of my dad, how he lived, and how he died. All the world should be able to look at a Christian person's life and death—like Dad's—as evidence of the pursuit and reflection of Jesus. I did.

Aslan's Country Vol. 1

Later the night of Dad's death, as the hurricane of heartache was pounding, there was still something that kept reminding me of my dreamlike vision earlier that night, the vision of Dad glowing with the eternal glow of new life. The vision wouldn't go away—the best way I could express it was that hope wouldn't leave me alone. The good-guy magic, hope, was speaking louder than my fear, louder than my mourning heart.

It was as if the sun came out and Aslan was offering his reassuring roar from within my heart. Good-guy magic had won. Good-guy magic would *always* win.

Maybe I was crazy, but I'd take that new kind of crazy over the desperation of Hypomania Land, spiritual sinfulness, a wrecked body born from the fear of mental disorder, and the deathly chaos of bitterness. I knew those kinds of *crazy* all too well.

It was only a daydream from a soul that was mourning, yet I knew with confidence that heroic worship *had* passed the test. The gates of Aslan's Country were ahead for all heroic worshipers of Jesus Christ, the Great Hero, the Heroic King! I knew I could confidently hope for, as Hebrews 11:16 called it, "a better country, a heavenly one."

Aslan's Country was *no* daydream.

Aslan's Country Vol. 2

Eternity—Aslan's Country—would be the inheritance of the heroic worshiper. It was a place fear could not exist, the place where hope extended into infinity—it was a place worth every effort to achieve.

> "My own plans are made. While I can, I sail east in the Dawn Treader. When she fails me, I paddle east in my coracle. When she sinks, I shall swim east with my four paws. And when I can swim no longer, if I have not reached

Aslan's Country, or shot over the edge of the world in
some vast cataract, I shall sink with my nose to the sunrise
and Peepiceek will be head of the talking mice in Narnia."
—Reepicheep the mouse; Voyage of the Dawn Treader, C.
S. Lewis, 1952

Driven by a vision of eternity since he was an infant, these were
the heroic lengths the champion mouse leader of all the mice in Narnia,
Reepicheep, would go to follow Aslan into his eternal country—it was this
very something in the personality and nature of Reepicheep that connected
with my heart.

*Reepicheep's vision and drive to achieve Aslan's Country was a poetic
reminder I needed to* **remain determined** *as a heroic worshiper.*

Reepicheep was guided continuously onward by the selfless, obedient, and adventurous service he would offer the good creatures of Narnia
and his king, Aslan. Because he understood the context of his life, depression and despair could not creep in! And that was Reepicheep's greatest
virtue, one which came as the result of heroic worship.

For my life here in the real world, humble, selfless, and obedient service remained the greatest evidence of my heroic worship, but the opposite
was also true; if I didn't know my correct context like Reepicheep did, I
wouldn't order my life's priorities and goals appropriately. Correct context *was everything* to my witness—it would *always* be everything. A silly
mouse in a fantasy story written by some dead guy (C.S. Lewis) helped me
understand my correct context even more completely.

But something else had struck me, too. In a wonderfully curious way,
Reepicheep reminded me a lot of my dad. And that was a joyful connection
for me to consider. No, Reepicheep didn't carry a badge that read "HERO,"
although maybe, as I imagined with my dad, it wouldn't have surprised me
if Reepicheep had an invisible HERO deputy badge fastened to his hairy
mouse chest . . .

The Wonder

"I never lost faith in the end of the story."
—Admiral James Stockdale, highest-ranking prisoner
of war in Vietnam

Heroic worship made it possible for me to know Dad's story was connected to the Great Storyteller's divine and eternal purpose. Dad knew his quest was not a cosmic accident or game. Dad knew he was a part of something far beyond the reaches of astonishment. What I'm saying is, Dad didn't lose faith in the end of the story either. And just like it did for my dad, heroic worship *was* what galvanized my faith here in the Shadowlands as well.

My pursuit and reflection of Jesus—my heroic worship—subdued the violent bipolar emotional shifts I used to endure. Everything in my life kept pointing back to Jesus: the altered living, my dedication to medication, accepting good enough, changing the rules, and knowing it takes everything—all of it, the entire quest—even aspects of my heroic Frankenstein—illuminated the path of heroic worship. Jesus Christ's heroic worship became my context and my witness; heroic as Jesus is heroic.

Throughout the story my dad and I shared, Jesus proved heroic worship was directly connected to eternity's endless wonder and adventure. Eternity was *not* going to be some lame and tame merry-go-round—no, Aslan's Country was going to be exhilarating for the heroic worshiper! Because of the Great Hero's wondrous infinite service and one-time sacrifice, Jesus proved selfless obedient service would always be the royal glory of the heroic worshiper. My fears of harps and clouds and naked chubby angels could kiss off. Instead, *certain* hope reopened the gates to the Garden.

". . . the more we know Jesus, the greater the wonder becomes . . .
not only in time, but also in eternity."
—Notes of William Barclay, Barclay's Daily Study Bible

The Garden Gates

Finally, one last story within a story. At the end of the concluding tale in *The Chronicles of Narnia* series, *The Last Battle*, every virtuous and noble follower of the great lion approached the garden of Aslan's Country together. At the garden's gate, the heroic worshiper Reepicheep, the ferocious yet chivalrous warrior mouse, stood as tall as he could to greet all of Narnia's heroes.

I have always loved the whimsical but potent and truly heroic imagery C. S. Lewis painted in my imagination—I guess I loved it enough I dreamed about it.

One early morning, between sleep and wake, I had a hope-filled dream that my dad would play the same role as Reepicheep in my family's story—it became an expectation, really. Still, I had even more dreams; I dreamed I would be allowed to extend the same loving welcome to my family when it was my turn. My third dream was that my children would choose the same honor and truly heroic duty to be a witness in life, and to greet their families and friends at the gates of Aslan's Country in death, just as their grandfather and father chose before them. And so on, and so on, and so on . . .

I longed for the endless odyssey it would be to pursue and reflect Jesus as a habit leading to hope in Aslan's Country, too! I longed for the unfurling mysteries of boundless adventures that awaited me, a heroic worshiper, for it would be my dauntless eternal destiny to love as Jesus loves and have nothing to fear—to be heroic like Him.

"Do you see what this means—all these pioneers who blazed the way, all these veterans cheering us on? It means we'd better get on with it. Strip down, start running—and never quit! No extra spiritual fat, no parasitic sins. Keep your eyes on Jesus, who both began and finished this race we're in. Study how He did it. Because He never lost sight of where He was headed—that exhilarating finish in and with God . . . That will shoot adrenaline into your souls!" —Hebrews 12:1–3, MSG

YOUR HEROIC QUEST

Begin your personal heroic worship journey and link your story with the great story of redemption by visiting Worship Hero on YouTube, Facebook, and worshiphero.com—join the community!

What Is Worship Hero?

Worship Hero is a small nonprofit storytelling studio that creates educational videos, study guides, and inspirational music to help people prepare and participate in a lifestyle of heroic worship. We develop tools to lead people to "Pursue Jesus. Reflect Jesus" as a habit leading to hope, not to become theologians but to live stories as heroic worshipers. We do this by focusing on stories from the Holy Bible and each other's heroic quests with Jesus. We are committed to understanding heroic worship in the correct context of the everlasting Holy Trinity while also communicating His eternal hope-filled nature to the modern world. By properly linking the heroic quest to a lifestyle of true worship, we mean to change how people understand and practice worship.

Our Mission

Change how people understand and practice worship by creating tools to "Pursue Jesus. Reflect Jesus." as a habit leading to hope.

Our Vision

Inspire people to mold their habits and talents around a vision of new life and endless adventure.

HEROIC DisGRACE